THE ACCIDENT:
A BIKE, A TRUCK, AND A TRAIN

Steve and Lori
 Your friendship means the world to me. Thank you for listening, thank you for being there.
   Hope you enjoy the book

        Chris

CHRIS DIKES

THE ACCIDENT:
A BIKE, A TRUCK, AND A TRAIN

CHRIS DIKES

ISBN: 978-1468193312
ISBN: 1468193317

Copyright © 2012 Chris Dikes

All rights reserved. No part of this book may be reproduced, transmitted, or stored in any form or by any means without the written permission of the author, except in the case of brief quotations embodied in critical articles and reviews.

Any trademarks, service marks, product names, or named features are assumed to be the property of their respective owners and are used only for reference.

The opinions expressed in this book are solely those of the author. The names of some individuals in this book have been changed. The conversations and order of events depicted are as the author remembers them.

TABLE OF CONTENTS

PROLOGUE	11
ONE: THE ACCIDENT	17
TWO: THE FIRST DAY	37
THREE: THE FIRST NIGHT	45
FOUR: THE FIRST WEEK	55
FIVE: THIS IS LUCKY?	65
SIX: FORWARD OR BACKWARD?	77
SEVEN: SETTLING THE BILL	97
ACKNOWLEDGEMENTS	103
ABOUT THE AUTHOR	105

For Angela, my wife, and Samuel, my son.

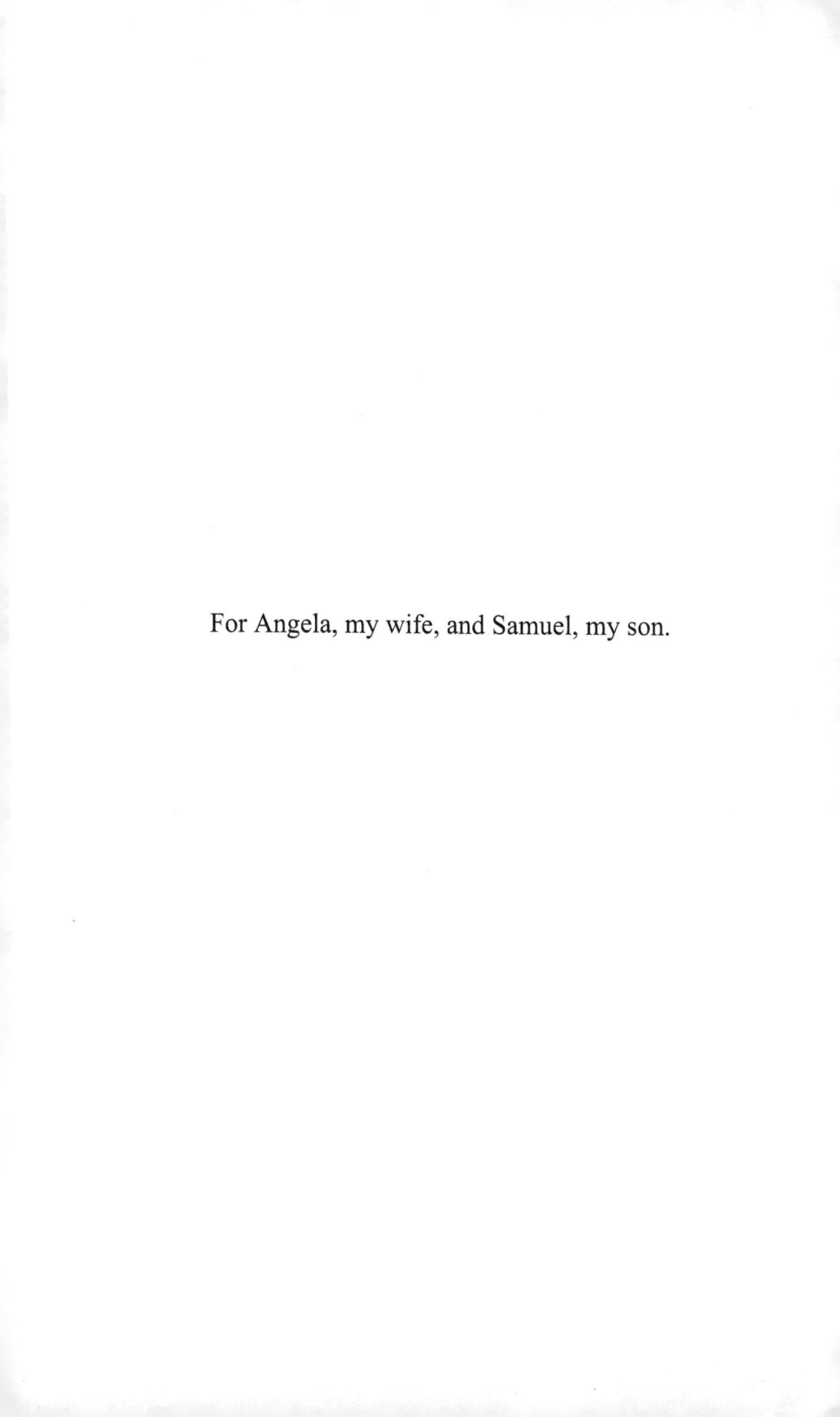

"Fear is not a bad place to start a spiritual journey. If you know what makes you afraid, you can see more clearly that the way out is through the fear."
Kathleen Norris, *Dakota*

PROLOGUE

My eyes opened and I gazed up at a white, metal ceiling. Where was I? How did I get here, wherever here was? What day was it? What time was it? Unable to figure out the answers to these questions, panic ensued and my heart started pounding. I tried to get up, but I couldn't. Both of my arms and legs had been strapped down to whatever I was laying on.

I noticed a woman in a blue uniform to my right.

"What happened?" I asked.

"You were in an accident."

Those words, "You were in an accident," released the pain from whatever gate had held it back. My face felt as if I'd been punched repeatedly, not that I'd ever been punched in the face multiple times, but this was what it must feel like. My chin throbbed. I tasted blood in my mouth and ran my tongue along my swollen lip. My neck had been placed in a brace to prevent me from moving my head in any direction. I couldn't see my left leg, but it felt as if it were burning and being hit with a baseball bat at the same time. To my right, I saw a sea of blood that covered the entirety of my right arm.

I closed my eyes and tried to remember anything. What was the last thing I remembered doing? I waited, but nothing came to mind. My thoughts were a blank slate. I opened my eyes and saw a picture of myself on a bike. Had I been riding my bike?

Had I been in some sort of accident while riding my bike?

To ride a bike is to accept the fact that at some point an accident will occur. The severity may vary from person to person and incident to incident, but escaping accident-free is not an option. Our family photo album contains a picture of me at my sixth birthday party. I am standing next to my new bike, a Huffy 56, and there is a huge smile on across my face. Grandpa Elkins and Uncle John stand on either side of me. I wonder if they were the ones who'd purchased the bike or if they just happened to be standing next to me for the picture. Behind us in the picture, there are people eating my birthday cake. All I care about is the bike. I don't remember the picture being taken, but I do remember taking that bike into the front of the house and trying to ride it in the street. I fell and scraped my elbows and knees. Welcome to the world of riding a bike.

  A few years later, after my parent's divorce and a series of moves, I moved with Mom to Seguin, Texas. During the summers, I rode my bike all over town. It was a different time in 1979, one where a fourth grader could disappear for the day on his bike. I used to ride my bike along the sidewalks of Texas Lutheran College. One afternoon, I thought I'd try to impress a couple of the college girls who were enrolled in summer school. After all, what nineteen-year-old girl wouldn't be impressed by a fourth grader on a bike who could ride like the wind? I sped up, hopped off the sidewalk onto the grass, passed the young women, and then attempted to hop back on the sidewalk. Instead of a graceful reentry, my front tire hit the edge of the sidewalk and catapulted me forward over the handlebars. I flew across the sidewalk and slid across the grass, scraping the inside of my right wrist. How I didn't injure myself further is beyond me. The girls walked by without even stopping to render aid. I guess we were not meant to be.

  Two weeks later, not having learned my lesson, I attempted to impress another group of college coeds with the same maneuver. The results were the same, except that this time I scraped the inside of my left wrist. For years, I had identical scars on each wrist.

  Throughout junior high, there would be more accidents and more scrapes, but once I turned sixteen and got a car, I left the bike in the garage. I took up biking in college, not so much for the exercise or the fun, but as a way to save money on gas. I rode to school and back, safely and without incident. Once my finances improved, I went back to the car.

In my mid-thirties, tired of running for exercise, I took up road cycling. Two weeks after the purchase of my first road bike, a red Trek 1200, and four weeks before the birth of my son, I sped away from a group of friends, hit a patch of gravel on a downhill turn, and sailed over the handlebars landing on my left shoulder in a patch of grass. I sat on the ground in a daze waiting for the others to catch up. Feeling okay, not seeing any bones sticking out through the skin or any blood on my body, I stood up and checked the bike for damages. It had survived as well. My shoulder felt stiff from landing on it and I noticed a slight bump that I didn't recall feeling before. Since I could still move my arm, I hopped on the bike and kept riding. When I arrived back at the car, my shoulder had stiffened to the point where I could barely move my arm and the pain had increased substantially. One of the riders in the group was a chiropractor who bought me a sling at CVS to immobilize the arm. We later went to his office where he took an x-ray of my shoulder and then advised me to see an orthopedist.

    I made an appointment with Dr. M, an orthopedist who specialized in sports medicine. In thirteen years of marriage, Angela, my very pregnant wife who tolerated my sports activities, had never been with me to a single doctor's appointment. Four weeks from her due date, she went with me, worried that Dr. M might prescribe surgery and she'd be stuck taking care of our newborn son and me.

    He diagnosed the injury as a grade three shoulder separation. "No surgery necessary, just physical therapy. He should be healed up in time for the birth of your son," he told her.

    I did everything the therapist told me to do and was back to normal by the time Samuel arrived.

Eighteen months later, riding into a cold headwind on a November morning, I rode up a hill on a deserted country road. A stray dog chased me up the hill and then lunged at my foot before I could escape. I thought the dog had missed biting me until I stopped to refill my water bottles ten miles later. The dog had nicked me just above my ankle, barely breaking the skin. There wasn't even a trickle of blood. I was more upset that the dog had ripped a hole in my new leg warmers. When I arrived home, I showed the minuscule bite to Angela.

"What do you think about this?" I asked.

"It doesn't look too bad."

"I guess so. They can probably be patched."

She looked at me with a furrowed brow. "I meant your leg."

"Oh yeah. Do you think I should do anything about it?"

"I don't know. Did the dog even break the skin?"

That night I decided to visit an emergency care clinic. I explained the injury to the attendant at the front counter, who took my name and handed me a stack of forms to fill out.

"All these?" I asked.

"Two are general client forms. The rest of that stack is for the dog bite. We're required to report all animal bites to the Department of Health and Human Services."

I should've stayed home, I thought. I found an empty seat and started filling out the forms. Twenty minutes later, a nurse called me back. She looked at the wound and asked how it had occurred. When the doctor arrived ten minutes later, he asked all the same questions.

"Well, the chances of you getting rabies from this are a million to one. You just need a tetanus shot," the doctor said.

I nodded my head. He was the doctor.

The nurse returned after the doctor left, cleaned the wound, and gave me a tetanus shot. I went home and thought nothing more about the incident.

Until Monday afternoon.

I worked for an investment firm, Fortune Financial Services, in Dallas and at four o'clock I sat in front of a computer preparing reports for a meeting later that week. My cellphone rang, but I didn't recognize the number on the caller id display. I considered ignoring the call, but then changed my mind and answered it.

"Chris Dikes?" the caller asked.

"Speaking."

"This is Debbie with the Department of Health and Human Services. Have you found the dog that bit you?"

"Found it? I haven't even looked for it. I don't even know if I could find it. I was on a bike on some deserted county road outside of Mansfield or Lillian."

"Do you know what happens if you do get rabies?"

"Not really, but I went to the doctor on Saturday night. He said not to worry about rabies. The dog barely broke the skin."

"Do you know what happens if you do get rabies?"

I thought I'd already answered that question. Maybe she hadn't heard me. "Not really."

"You die." She then explained in graphic detail how I would die if indeed this mangy mutt had transmitted rabies to me. "I don't know what you're doing at work and I don't know what that quack of a doctor told you, but if you can't find that dog, you'd better see your primary care physician and get a second opinion."

I bolted out of the office, sped down the highway an hour south to Mansfield, driving up and down what I thought were the same roads I'd ridden on Saturday. Country roads all look alike. Ranch houses, trailer homes, and lots of flat land. While I drove, I called my doctor and scheduled an appointment for the following morning. After two hours, I called off the unsuccessful search.

The next morning, the doctor took one look at the wound and prescribed rabies shots. "Better safe than sorry." At least they didn't give them in the stomach anymore. That's the first question people ask when they find out I got rabies shots. On the first day, I was supposed to receive four injections but ended up getting eleven or so. I lost count. One shot was intended for the wound, but since there was no flesh above the ankle, she had to inject, withdraw, and re-inject multiple times. I returned to the doctor four more times over the next month for more shots.

Two years passed before the next accident. On a cold and wet December day, I went for a ride. On this particular road, there was a ninety-degree turn. One second I was sitting upright on the bike and the next I was sliding across the pavement disengaged from the bike. I came to a stop in the middle of the road while the bike continued across the street and into a ditch. I emerged with torn clothing and a bunch of cuts and abrasions, but no breaks or separations.

In each of these accidents, I knew every detail of what had happened. But looking up at the white ceiling of the ambulance, I had no idea what had taken place or how badly I might be injured.

ONE
THE ACCIDENT

August 11, 2009.
A Tuesday morning.
The alarm went off at six a.m. and I got out of bed. After I changed into my cycling clothes, I tiptoed downstairs, careful not to wake Samuel, our three-year-old son who awoke at the slightest noises. I filled up two water bottles and aired up the tires on my bike, a Trek Madone 5.1. Before leaving, I checked my rear jersey pockets to make sure I'd grabbed my wallet, cellphone, and keys.

Four weeks prior, Dr. M's assistant had cleared me to resume riding a bike after a lengthy struggle with tendonitis. His instructions to me were, "Work back slowly. Don't overdue the intensity or the duration of your rides." I interpreted "work back slowly" as five one-hour rides per week, one two-hour ride on the weekend, and one day off. For those one-hour rides, I circled a five-mile loop around my neighborhood as fast as I could. "Intensity" could also be interpreted many different ways.

This loop took me past Young Junior High and Martin High School. The previous morning, I'd noticed an increase in the traffic around the high school. When I checked the district website that afternoon, I learned that school would be starting the following week. I decided that this would be my last week of early morning rides. I'd have to find another way or place to get in my time on the bike. Teenage drivers, late-for-work parents, and oh-no-this-school-zone-is-slowing-me-down drivers don't make for the safest riding conditions.

I approached Martin High School as I completed the second loop that morning. I turned right on Pleasant Ridge, a four lane road, and after I turned I looked behind me to check the oncoming traffic. I saw a line of cars at the light so I turned into the student parking lot rather than continuing straight on the road.

In all the times I'd ridden by Martin High School, I'd never turned into the parking lot. Ever. But something in my gut made me uneasy about the traffic so I opted to trust my instincts and deviate from my normal routine. I pedaled in small circles while I watched the traffic. I congratulated myself on being safety conscious. For once, I'd not plowed ahead without consideration of the risks involved. I looked at the clock and calculated that if I pushed hard I could make one more loop before I needed to be home.

I re-entered Pleasant Ridge and turned right. Again, I looked back over my left shoulder at the oncoming traffic and counted three cars stopped at the light behind me, all of them in the right hand lane, the same lane as me. I placed my hands on the top of the handlebars and moved over to the far right side of the right lane. Each car sped up, moved over to the left lane, and passed me. I counted all three and then I relaxed as I concentrated on riding up the incline on Pleasant Ridge. I passed the entrance to my neighborhood and dismissed the idea of turning in. I could get one more loop in.

That is the last thing I remember.

The next memory I have is waking up in the back of an ambulance.

I don't know what happened in those forty minutes. Anything I know has come from eyewitness accounts and police reports. From those, I learned the following; a man driving a Ford Ranger pickup truck hit me from behind. He told the police he never saw me until he hit me. I was not knocked unconscious, but I remember nothing of the accident or the aftermath.

Absolutely nothing.

Zip. Zilch. Nada.

"What if?" was one of my first thoughts. What if I hadn't gone riding that morning? What if I'd left earlier or later? What if I hadn't pulled into the student parking lot? I had never done that in all the times I'd ridden on Pleasant Ridge. What if I'd circled the parking lot fewer times or more times? What if when I passed my neighborhood, I'd opted to go home instead of trying to get one more loop in? What if this? What if that?

Why had my instincts led me astray? If I'd done what I always did and pressed on without going into the parking lot, I'd have been at home eating breakfast instead of lying in the back of an ambulance?

What if?

"What happened?" I asked.
"You've been in an accident," the woman answered, "We're taking you to the hospital."
"Oh." How badly had I been injured? Was I going to be okay? Was this woman not telling me things about the injuries or the accident? Why had they immobilized me? Was I paralyzed?

"Hello," the woman said. I turned my eyes from the ceiling to the ambulance's back door and saw Angela getting in.

How did she know I'd been in an accident?

Although I thought I'd just woken up, I later learned that I'd been awake the whole time. One of the witnesses called 911 and another retrieved my cellphone from my rear jersey pocket and called Angela. I was alert enough to give them the password to my phone and then tell them whom to call. But I don't remember any of that. I remember passing the street into my neighborhood and then being in the ambulance.

Angela sat next to me on one of the benches while the EMS technician prepared to transport me to the hospital. Angela has a history of passing out at the sight of blood, no

19

matter how small or great the quantity, but to her credit, at the sight of all my blood, she stayed upright.

"I dropped Samuel off at the neighbor's. I'm parked across the street and I've already called..."

I faded out for a minute, struggling to concentrate on the blast of information she was giving me. I didn't even know what street I was on.

"You're taking him to Medical Center of Arlington, right?" Angela asked. Medical Center of Arlington was ten minutes from our house.

"No, JPS," the technician replied, "All head traumas go to JPS." JPS was located near downtown Fort Worth, thirty minutes from our house.

Head trauma? What did she mean by head trauma? I'd hit my head? Was that why they'd put me in this neck brace?

A fireman stepped into the crowded ambulance. "What would you like us to do with your bike?"

"Um." Words were jumbled in my head and I couldn't spit them out.

The fireman turned his gaze from me and looked to Angela. I suspect she might've had a few suggestions- burn it, trash it, destroy it, or somehow make it permanently disappear. She didn't say anything either.

"How about we take it to the station?" he asked.

Angela nodded her head and I may have blinked twice. Either way, he jumped out of the ambulance to take care of my bike.

"Time to go," the EMS technician declared.

Angela planned to follow the ambulance in her car, but the police had blocked traffic in both directions. Once the ambulance left, they began to unwind the traffic jam, but she was prevented from following the ambulance. Sitting in traffic, Angela called everyone she could think of to get directions to JPS.

On this day, I hoped she remembered the part of our marriage vows that said "for better or for worse."

The technician slammed the doors shut and double-checked the gurney to make sure I was secured. "Can't have you rolling around back here," she said.

I guess it helped her to have a sense of humor.

The driver turned on the siren and sped off towards the hospital. As soon as we left, I started shivering.

"Are you cold?" she asked.

"Yeah," I mumbled. Whatever had happened to my lip, talking made it hurt.

The technician covered me in blankets before she radioed the JPS ER to inform them that we were on our way. As she described my injuries, she mentioned "possible concussion." She then inserted an IV into my left arm.

She moved around to my right side and sat next to me. "I need to cut off your clothes to check for any additional injuries. Is that okay with you?"

What could I say? No, I don't want to know if anything else is wrong? I grunted an approval. She grabbed a pair of scissors and I resumed staring at the ceiling. I could feel tears welling up inside me. I was supposed to be at work by now, not lying in the back of an ambulance being stripped of my clothes. I was careful, how did I end up in an accident? This wasn't fair. This wasn't right. Tears eked out the side of my eyes and snot slid out of my nose. Since both my arms were strapped to the gurney I couldn't wipe either away.

The technician noticed the tears sliding down my face. "Why are you crying?"

I want to believe that she meant well. Had she cut me with the scissors? Had the pain increased exponentially? Had something changed with my condition? But even though she probably meant well, her question infuriated me. Wasn't I allowed to cry at a time like this? Wouldn't she be crying if she were lying here, freezing, suffering in pain, and fearful of what the doctors might tell you?

But as much as I wanted to let out the anger that she'd triggered, as much as I wanted to yell at her, my busted lip made even whispering difficult. Besides, if I yelled at her, at some point in the drive to the ER, she might ask what I did for a living, and I'd have to tell her the truth, "I'm a pastor."

I ignored her question and clenched my jaw. The tears dried and the snot mingled with the blood.

Trips to the emergency room were a rare occurrence for me. After my parents divorced, Mom and Dad moved to separate apartment complexes. We lived with Mom and visited Dad every other weekend. One Sunday afternoon, Jason, my younger brother, and I were playing football in the parking lot and the football sailed over the wooden privacy fence that separated the apartments from an abandoned field.

I noticed that someone had already knocked down one of the wooden planks. "Jason, I'll go through the hole and get the ball." I stepped through that hole onto a board in the overgrown grass, which obscured an erect nail. My foot landed directly on that nail. I screamed and then yelled for Jason to get Dad. He took me to the emergency room for my first tetanus shot.

A couple of years later, my step-dad, Tom, purchased a mini-bike. Initially, he forbade me from riding it, but I begged and pleaded for the chance.

"But, you can only ride it in the backyard," he said when he relented.

Presumably this would be safer than the street. On either side of our backyard was a chain link fence, but along the back was a wooden privacy fence so we wouldn't have to look at the gas station behind us. Tom stood next to me with a cup of coffee in one hand and a cigarette in the other. He gave me a two-minute tutorial, which consisted of him pointing out where the gas and brakes were. I hopped on the mini-bike, not wearing a helmet, and sped off. I headed for the corner where the two fences intersected. They told me later that rather than using the brakes I kept throttling the gas and going faster. Instead of running into the two fences, I hit a hole in the yard that flipped me in the air and I landed on my right shoulder. Instead of rolling about in pain, I jumped up and ran into the house screaming and cursing.

I wasn't a pastor then.

For two hours, I knelt on the floor next to my bed crying in pain. When I failed to stop, Mom and Tom decided that something might be wrong with me. We got in the car and drove across the street to the hospital emergency room. Across the street. The x-ray showed a broken collarbone. Six weeks in a sling.

I managed to stay away from ER's until high school, when I'd gone roller-skating on a Saturday night. I'd skated competitively for four years and had worked in a skating rink for Tom. I lost count of the number of times I'd fallen, run into railings and even walls, all without breaking a bone. On this night, I tripped over my skates and extended my right arm to soften the fall. I landed awkwardly and rolled over feeling immense pain in my right arm. When I stood up, I had to use my left arm to pick up the right. The manager called my Dad to come get me while someone else removed my skates for me. In the ER, after a series of x-rays, the doctor informed us that I'd broken both bones in my right arm.

"Clean and complete break," he said. "And the bones have slid under one another as well. We're going to have to sedate you in order to set the bones."

I stayed in the hospital for a week.

In all of my visits, I managed to get there without the help of an ambulance. Until that Tuesday on August 11th.

If there can be any upside to a possible head trauma, then it's getting to bypass everyone else in the ER waiting room. The downside of this express service is the head trauma itself. We arrived at the JPS ER and the driver opened the back of the ambulance where a team of nurses and doctors met us. The EMS technician once more relayed information about the accident as well as what she'd done in the back of the ambulance. She might as well have been talking in a foreign language as nothing she said made any sense to me. The medical team wheeled me down a hallway and into an examination room where they transferred me onto a hospital bed. Either I'd lost my glasses in the accident or someone had removed them afterwards, but with my poor vision, I couldn't make out anyone's face. Everything was a blur.

"I put all your stuff from the accident, including your clothes, in this bag," the EMS technician told me. "I'm going to leave it on the floor next to the wall."

The doctors and nurses spoke to one another and periodically directed their questions to me. "Does that hurt?" "Does this hurt?" and "Are you allergic to any medications?" The doctor, who never bothered to introduce himself, ordered a battery of tests. Then they rolled me on my side, exposing my naked backside to everyone, presumably so they could check for any injuries on my back.

"Just abrasions," someone said.

Just abrasions.

They gently let me down on my back and I noticed a nurse to my left grab my IV line and inject something. Within seconds, a burning sensation rushed through my entire body and my vision started going black. The room began to spin.

"What's happening to me? I don't feel very good." I attempted to sit up, thinking that I might feel better. Nurses on both sides of me placed a hand on my shoulder to keep me in place. They didn't have to bother, as I couldn't lift my head higher than an inch off the bed.

"It's morphine. For the pain. It'll pass in a moment," she said.

When the radiology technician arrived, everyone departed the room. Rather than wheel me down to the x-ray room, this particular exam room had been fitted with x-ray equipment. I continued to alternate between sweating and freezing. When I froze, my body shivered and shook.

"Please keep still," the radiology technician told me.

"I'm trying."

When she finished and departed, another nurse appeared. "Time for a CAT scan," she said and wheeled me down the hallway to another department. I lay there on the bed outside the room while the employees discussed their lunch plans and a movie a couple of them had seen. When they were finished, two of them retrieved me for the CAT scan. They reviewed the order sheet and debated among themselves whether or not a particular test should've been ordered as well. Unable to reach a consensus, they asked me what the doctor had ordered.

"I don't know," I mumbled.

One of them called the nurse who talked to the doctor who clarified what he wanted. He did want that particular test. The one who'd questioned the initial order gloated to the others.

Please get this over with, I thought to myself.

When they finished with the CAT scan, someone else wheeled me back to my exam room where Angela was waiting for me. For the first time that morning, we were alone.

I could barely talk with a busted lip and I didn't have the energy to engage in much of a conversation.

"Do you know what happened?" she asked.

"I don't remember."

We changed the subject to Samuel and how he might react.

"He didn't seem fazed by the fact that you were in an accident, but he might be a little freaked out when he sees you," Angela said.

"He's probably having the time of his life at the neighbor's," I said.

My boss, Joe, the pastor at CrossRoads of Arlington Church where I worked, entered the room. Angela had called him. "I can't believe this happened," he said.

Join the club.

After he left, it was once again Angela and myself. The room they'd placed me in was across the hall from the nurse's station, which contained the radio where EMS technicians communicated with the ER about the patients they were bringing in. The volume seemed to be set as high as possible and we could listen in on every conversation. The radio calls gave Angela and I something to talk about rather than my accident. It also let me know how far down the chart of priorities I was falling.

"Motorcycle and car accident. Individual not wearing a helmet."

"Heroin overdose. Non-responsive."

"Head-on collision. Not wearing a seatbelt."

A nurse stopped by the room. "It's been a crazy morning. We haven't forgotten about you." She turned to leave the room, but then stopped and looked back at me. "You were very lucky."

Lucky? I didn't feel lucky and lucky didn't tell me a whole lot about my condition. So far, they'd done nothing but check me out and take lots of tests. Lucky could be taken a number of different ways. Lucky to be alive. Lucky that I wasn't paralyzed. Lucky that it would only take five to ten years for me to recover. Lucky that I'd be released within the hour.

I wanted to say, "Define lucky," but she'd already left the room.

"Am I supposed to be tasting that liquid?" I asked.

Angela had gone to the lobby to call family and friends with an update, I'd survived but we didn't know anything else. She'd tried to call from inside the ER, but there was no cell reception. As soon as she'd left, a male nursed entered the room with orders to stitch up the hole underneath my lip.

He sat down next to me and said, "First, I'm going to pour this liquid over the wound to clean and disinfect the area." When I questioned tasting the liquid inside my mouth, he leaned over and inspected the wound closer. "That's a through and through. Good to know, not that we do anything about the inside. It'll heal on its own. Eventually." He numbed the area near the wound with an injection before he started sewing.

When he left, the doctor entered the room. "All your tests and scans are coming back normal. That's good. You appear to be free of any internal or life-threatening injuries. However, the x-rays of your left leg, specifically your calf, show that you have a divot fracture on your fibula. The radiologist can't determine if this is the result of an old injury or if you sustained it in today's accident. Have you injured your left fibula previously?"

"No."

"Are you feeling any discomfort in your left leg?" He pushed aside the sheets that covered my left leg.

Discomfort would be an understatement of what I felt. I wished I felt discomfort rather than the throbbing fire of pain than engulfed my leg. "My lower left leg is killing me. It. Hurts. Bad."

"Well, that's pretty normal. You did get hit by a truck. There should be some pain."

"It. Hurts. Really. Bad."

Since I still didn't have any glasses, I couldn't tell if his expression had changed at all. My left leg had never hurt like this before, so I doubted that the divot fracture was the result of a previous injury. I would never forget pain like this. I decided to sit up and point to the area on my leg where I felt the pain. With many grunts, I lifted my head and reached towards my left leg with my left arm.

Bad idea. Very bad idea.

As soon as I lifted my head, the room began to spin. As it spun faster and faster, I dropped back onto the bed. Every pore of my body opened up and sweat drenched the gown they'd placed over my naked body earlier. Nausea engulfed my stomach and I thought I might throw up. I closed my eyes and clinched my fists, wondering what was happening and wishing everything would stop. I heard shoes squeak on the floor and opened my eyes to see nurses rushing into my room. One of them injected something into my IV. The doctor turned and walked out of the room while one of the nurses stayed with me. Angela returned in time to witness the commotion. A few minutes passed before the spinning and nausea subsided.

    This is lucky? I closed my eyes again. What were they not telling me? What did they not know? Was I going to be okay? Would I be able to hold Angela again? Play with Samuel? Resume my job? Would I even be able to sit up again?

    We waited for someone, a doctor or a nurse, to tell us something. Nobody had indicated if they'd be keeping me overnight or sending me home. Should Angela go eat lunch or would we be leaving soon?

    While we waited, I sensed an urgent need to use the bathroom. This surprised me since I'd hadn't eaten anything and the only thing I'd had to drink was a half a bottle of water while riding my bike. Maybe they'd put something in the IV. Whatever the cause, I needed to pee. Angela found a nurse and passed on my request.

    "They'll be here in a minute," she said, "They're taking care of another emergency."

    It took longer than a minute, more like ten, maybe even twenty. When the nurse arrived, my need had become an emergency and she gave me two options. "You can go in a bucket, or we can help you out of bed and let you walk to the bathroom across the hallway." From her dismissive tone of the first option and cheery offer of the second, I surmised that she wanted me to get out of bed and walk. I don't blame her. I wouldn't want to deal with a bucket of urine either.

    But my leg throbbed. Every time I tried to sit up the room spun away from me.

    "I don't know."

"We'll help you up out of bed and walk with you to the bathroom."

I took a deep breath. This might be some kind of test. If I could get up and walk to the bathroom without falling over, then they might let me go home today. If I couldn't, then they might keep me overnight. I could handle a little pain. "Get me up."

The nurse pushed a button that slowly raised the head of the bed so that I went from laying down to sitting up. The room spun much less than when I'd tried to sit up myself. While I acclimated myself to being upright, she moved the IV stand from the left side of the bed to the right.

"Ready?" she asked.

I nodded my head and pushed my legs over the right side of the bed. I took a couple of deep breaths before gently sliding off the bed and letting my feet touch the floor. I leaned forward, placing my weight on my legs.

OH MY GODDDD!!!!!!!!!!! OH MY GOD!!!! Hot, burning, throbbing pain roared up and down my left leg. I ground my teeth and clenched my jaw. I grabbed a hold of the bed and squeezed it with both of my hands. I found the limit of the pain I could take and this was way past it.

The doctor's earlier words rang in my ears. "We're unable to determine if this fracture is the result of today's accident or a previous injury."

I had a theory.

I couldn't decide if I wanted to scream or cry. I stood there for a minute hoping that the pain might diminish after a minute. It didn't. Oh, and I really had to go to the bathroom.

I placed my right hand on the IV stand for support. As I walked, I leaned to my right hoping to keep as much weight as possible off of my left leg. The nurse pushed the stand and Angela walked on my left side. The pain increased rather than diminishing. I could feel it up and down the entire left side of my body. I inched my way out of the room and across the hallway.

"I need to stop." Sweat poured off me and I was out of breath. The nurse helped me sit down in a chair.

"What hurts?" the nurse asked.

"My left leg is killing me," I gasped.

I never wanted to get up out of that chair, but my bladder exerted its force. If I didn't get to a bathroom soon, I was going to lose control. Angela and the nurse helped me stand back up. When we arrived at the bathroom, the nurse sent Angela in with me. Just in case. We'd been married for sixteen years, so there wasn't anything she hadn't seen. When I finished, I leaned my left shoulder against the wall in the bathroom. The nausea had returned.

"What's wrong?" Angela asked.

"I think I might throw up," I replied, "and the room is spinning a lot."

"Don't move."

That I could do. Angela left me propped against the wall while she got the nurse. With one of them on either side of me, they guided me out of the bathroom and sat me down in an office chair that happened to be in the hallway.

"Can you walk back to your bed?" the nurse asked.

I shook my head no.

"Wait here, while I get a wheelchair."

The dizziness and sweating stopped, only to be replaced by the chills. They told me I was fine, but this didn't feel fine. This felt like hell. Again, were they not telling me something? Had the medical staff missed something?

"I can't find a wheelchair anywhere. How about if I just roll you along in this office chair? Can you lift your legs off the ground?"

I nodded my head but couldn't lift either of my legs. Angela and the nurse each lifted one of my feet onto the chair legs and then the nurse pushed me back to my room. My new companions, dizziness and nausea, made a return visit when I got back into the bed. I closed my eyes and tried to push everything out. Maybe I would go to sleep and wake up from this horrible nightmare.

The nurse returned a few minutes later. "The attending doctor has paged the on-call orthopedist to come and look at your leg and x-rays," she said, "He saw you trying to walk."

While I rested, Angela left again to phone our family and friends. We still didn't know anything. Angela decided, and I agreed, that her Mom would get Samuel from our neighbor's house. If they were going to release me that day, it would still be hours away. As soon as she left, the orthopedist arrived with someone following him.

"This is a medical student. Do you mind if he observes?" the orthopedist asked. He mentioned his name. I nodded my head and forgot.

"That's fine."

"I'm going to examine your left leg," he said, pushing the sheets aside and grabbing my leg. He lifted it a few feet off the bed, pushed it toward me, pulled it back, and then twisted it every which way. As soon as he touched my leg and began his machinations, the pain skyrocketed.

"Does that hurt?" he asked.

"Yes," I gasped.

"Hmm." He put my leg back on the bed and stared at it for a minute. "I'm going to order some more x-rays."

I told Angela about the orthopedist when she returned. "We're going to be here awhile longer."

Of the three of us, Samuel was having one of the best days. First, he spent all day playing at the neighbor's house and now his Mammaw would be picking him up.

Rather than take the x-rays in the room as they'd done earlier, the radiology technician wheeled me down the hallway and parked me outside the x-ray lab. I stared up at the ceiling, the only place I could look. I can only imagine how bored Angela must've been. When the lab became available, the technician wheeled me into the room, where I noticed a distinct difference in temperature. It was freezing and my body started to shiver. The technician twisted and turned my leg to get the picture she wanted. The leg torture generated some heat but that didn't stop the shivering.

"Hold it there. Don't move."

Easier said than done. The shivers were beyond my control.

When she finished, she pushed me back to the room and left us to wait even longer. Angela commented that the nurses brought the patient in the next room a sandwich. My stomach registered its desire for food with a gurgle of growls and grumbles.

"I wonder if they'll bring me something to eat," I said.

"That would be great. I'm starving," Angela replied.

"What time is it?"

"A little after three."

Nobody brought or even offered us lunch.

The orthopedist returned without his medical student. "You have a divot fracture in your left fibula."

"That's what they said this morning. What is a divot fracture?"

"It's like it sounds. In the force of the accident, something struck your fibula and chipped a piece of the bone off creating a divot. Since the fibula is the non-weight bearing bone in your calf, you'll be fine. You'll need to stay off it so that the bone can mend so I'm going to order the nurse to fit you with crutches. You'll probably be on them for about six weeks. I'd like you to follow up with me in about seven to ten days at my office so that we can make sure everything is healing fine. Once the nurses get you those crutches, you'll be discharged."

Discharged? As in going home? No overnight stay at the hospital? Yes!

The previously dormant activity in my room dissolved as nurses swarmed into my room. Since I wasn't dying or staying the night, I suppose they wanted this room for someone else. That someone could have it. One nurse asked my height so she could adjust the crutches. Another smothered my right arm in silver sulfadiazine cream and then wrapped it in gauze. She placed the remaining contents of the container in a bag for me. "This is the best stuff," she said. Someone else removed the IV and another picked up my bag of belongings that the EMS technician had left on the floor.

"Do you want your clothes?" someone asked.

I couldn't see them, but I knew they'd been covered in blood and cut off me. "No, you can throw them away."

Angela went outside again, this time to call her Mom. We'd decided that Samuel should stay at her Mom's for the night. Who knew what my first night at home might be like? It would be easier on everyone if he stayed there.

Another nurse presented me with seventeen pages of instructions for my care as well as three prescriptions from the doctor. She breezed through them and then asked me to initial each page and sign the last one. Most of what she said didn't make any sense, but I'd do whatever and sign whatever so that I could leave.

I handed her the pen. "By the way, do you have some shorts for me to wear?"

"What about your clothes?" she asked.

"They were cut off of me in the ambulance."

Surely, they had a pair of shorts or boxers. Something.

"Sorry, we don't have anything."

My exit would be as interesting as my entrance. I'd be leaving as naked as I entered. Well, I'd be leaving in a gown that didn't cover my backside.

"Let me find a wheelchair and then we'll have you on your way," a nurse told me.

The executives at JPS must've hidden the rash of wheelchair thefts from the local news. It took a nurse forty-five minutes to find a wheelchair in the ER. Angela left to bring her car around to the designated pickup spot. The nurse helped me out of the bed and into the wheelchair. She then handed me a couple of bed sheets to place over my lap.

"Just in case," she said.

Another weighed me down with crutches, copies of the papers I'd signed, a bag with silver sulfadiazine cream and gauze bandages, and another bag with items someone had collected from the scene of the accident.

"All right. We just need to stop at the billing department on our way out."

A billing clerk pushed a stack of papers in front of me. Without my glasses, I couldn't read them. Well, I could've if I'd bent over, but my body didn't feel like bending over. Every time I moved something hurt, so I chose to move as little as possible. The clerk pointed where she needed my initials and signature. I did as she wished.

She collected those forms from me and then handed me one final document to sign. "JPS does not have an agreement with your health insurance provider, which means that we can't accept your insurance as a form of payment. Please sign at the bottom acknowledging that you are responsible for the cost of all treatment and services rendered to you today."

I looked up at her. She pursed her lips and offered an apologetic smile.

I started to question the policy. A truck had hit me while I was riding my bike. The EMS technicians had given me no choice over the hospital they would take me to. I'd spent most of the day arguing with the doctor over the extent of my injuries. As much as I wanted to vent, I wanted to leave even more and if signing this form meant I could leave, then I'd sign it. I'd deal with the financial burden later.

The nurse wheeled me outside to the curb where we waited for Angela. It being an August afternoon in Texas, the temperature exceeded one hundred degrees. Sweat once more formed all over my body. The three blankets covering my lap were causing my legs to itch.

"Do you see her car?" the nurse asked.

I did my best to identify her white Toyota Avalon but without my glasses I couldn't see a thing. I pointed at the first white car I saw. My left arm throbbed when I lifted it and pointed. Somehow I'd picked out the right car. Angela stopped and the nurse opened the passenger door. The nurse took everything from my lap and put it in the backseat. Then she helped me into the front seat. I'm not sure if I managed to flash anyone and I didn't care if I did.

"Take care," she said before shutting the door.

I turned to Angela and said, "Let's get out of here."

TWO
THE FIRST NIGHT

    I leaned forward to look at the digital clock on the dashboard. "Four-thirty. I'm starving."
    "Me too. Where to?" Angela asked while navigating her way out of the JPS parking lot.
    "The first place you see." I reached down and moved the seat back. "But no McDonalds, Burger King, Taco Bell, Long John Silvers, Church's Fried Chicken, or anything like that."
    She ignored my comment and kept driving, possibly taking my food snobbery as an indicator that I'd begun to feel better. Yet, those were the only fast food restaurants we passed. We drove by a few sit down places like Chili's and Olive Garden, but without any underwear or shorts to cover my nether regions, those places weren't realistic options either. Not that I felt like going into a restaurant. I wanted a place with a drive through.
    "I'm sure there's something closer to home," I said. Besides, when you hadn't eaten all day what was thirty more minutes?
    I reached into the backseat and grabbed the plastic bag that contained my things from the accident. On top, I found my Rudy Project Exception glasses. They're prescription glasses with a flip-down sunglasses attachment made to withstand the rigors of sporting events. I wore them whenever I went cycling. I inspected the glasses and, except for a few small scratches to the frame, they appeared to have survived. The same could not be said for the sunglasses attachment, which I couldn't locate in the bag. I put the glasses on and could see clearly for the first time in hours. Further inside the bag, I found my wallet (now scuffed and torn) along with my keys. My cycling gloves were there as

well, albeit covered with my dried blood. I didn't remember them being removed from my hands. I saw my helmet near the bottom of the bag and pulled it out as well, running my fingers over the dents and scratches that indicated where my head had hit the ground that morning.

I looked up from the bag and stared out at the traffic. Within a couple of minutes, the nausea, dizziness, and sweating returned. I leaned forward and put my head in my lap as well as removed my glasses. "Stay in the right lane," I cautioned, "I might have to throw up."

The wave of illness subsided after a few moments, but when I sat back up sickness overwhelmed me again. Once more, I put my head back down. This routine continued a few more times before I gave up and kept my head down and eyes closed.

As we neared home, Angela turned into the drive through at Arby's. She ordered something for herself and I chose two roast beef sandwiches and a large Sprite. I figured those would be best for my seemingly sensitive stomach.

"Sure you don't want any curly fries?" Angela asked.

"Bland is best right now."

I took a sip of the Sprite, my first fluids of the day, and the sugary carbonation tasted so refreshing. I grabbed one of the sandwiches out of the bag. The smell of beef and toasted bread made my stomach growl with anticipation. Forgetting my condition, I opened my mouth wide to take a bite, which sent pain throbbing throughout my lip and chin. I put the sandwich down and bent over. I checked my face for blood with my hand, fearing that I might've ripped open the stitches, but I found none. When the pain subsided, I took a tiny nibble of the sandwich.

We turned into our neighborhood and I wondered how Samuel would react when he saw me. He tended to be fearful, so would my injuries exacerbate those fears? I put my half-eaten sandwich back in the bag.

Angela carried everything into the house while I hobbled in with the aid of my crutches. I went through the laundry room and abruptly stopped in the hallway, avoiding a near collision with Samuel, a blur of blond hair, as he ran by me. "Hey daddy," he yelled not even stopping to look at me.

Perhaps my fears about how he might react were overdone.

I went straight to the couch in the living room. Angela found Samuel in another room and ushered him back to where I sat. He'd never spent a night away from home so we expected that we might have to convince him, perhaps even bribe him, to stay with Mammaw for the evening.

"Samuel, do you want to spend the night at Mammaw's?" Angela asked.

"YEAHHHHH!!!!! Let's go," he hollered, jumping off the couch and running for the front door.

It appeared that we'd underestimated our own son. Angela chased after him and reminded him that before he could leave, they needed to pack a few things, like a change of clothes, some toys, and a toothbrush. The three of them went upstairs to pack Samuel's things while I remained on the couch, nibbling away at each of my two sandwiches.

When Samuel bounded down the stairs, he returned to the living room and stood in front of me. "Good night, Daddy," he said and stepped forward to give me a gentle hug and a kiss on my cheek. Then he ran to the door.

Before I left the ER, one of the nurses implored me to get my prescriptions filled. "As bad as you feel today, you're going to feel horrible tomorrow." Angela heard the nurse's instructions so after finishing her meal, she decided to go to the pharmacy to get all three prescriptions filled- an anti-inflammatory, a muscle relaxant, and a narcotic pain reliever, hydrocodone.

"I'm not taking the muscle relaxant or the pain reliever," I said. Having heard too many stories of people becoming addicted to hydrocodone, I feared the same for myself. Addiction ran in my family and if that tendency were a genetic trait, I wanted to stay as far away from it as possible. Besides, I hadn't liked the experience with morphine that morning. I figured I could tolerate the pain, no matter how bad it might get.

"Since you're going out," I continued, "would you mind picking up some magazines for me at Barnes and Noble?" Even though I had a stack of books to read, I tend to be a voracious reader, I figured that I'd be spending a lot of time sitting around so some magazines might be good to have as well. I almost hesitated in making the request, but she wouldn't have to go that far out of her way. Barnes and Noble was across the street from the pharmacy. "Feel free to get something for yourself as well," I added, as if that might seal the deal, as if she needed my permission, which she didn't.

She departed; leaving me alone for the first time that day and I wanted to do one thing, see the injuries. I'd caught glimpses of myself here and there, in the bathroom at the hospital and in the reflection of the car mirror, but those were brief. There'd been no time to study the injuries, to see what sort of damage had been inflicted on me.

I stood up with the help of the crutches and the room started to spin. I tightened my grip on the crutches, not moving in any direction, and hoping that if I fell it would be backwards onto the couch rather than forward onto the coffee table. The spinning eventually passed and I limped into the bathroom.

I turned and faced the mirror, looking first into my eyes, then to the various abrasions on my face. I lifted my head and glanced at the swelling on my chin, seeing an inch long gash there. My left arm was covered in cuts. A nurse had covered my right arm in gauze because of the abrasion that extended the entire length of my arm and I'd seen plenty of that already. My left thumb, in addition to being black and blue, had swollen to twice the size of my right. On my right thigh, I found a bruise the size of my palm. My left calf had swelled to three times my right and was also covered in cuts and bruises. One of the bruises on the backside of my calf was the exact shape of the pedal from my bike. Dirt and blood covered every part of my body. I even found dried blood in my ears.

  I didn't know whether to cry or to scream. I wanted to do both and tears formed in my eyes. Questions of why and how bounced around in my head as I stared at my reflection. Why me? Why now? What now? What do I do now? Not finding an answer, I shuffled back to the living room and dropped down onto the couch. I rested my left leg on the coffee table and turned on the TV.

  When Angela returned, I swallowed the anti-inflammatory pill she gave me and didn't ask where she put the other prescriptions.

  In our two-story house, the bedrooms are upstairs. There was a small room on the first floor, a mother-in-law suite the realtor called it, but we'd turned it into a playroom for Samuel. This meant that all the beds were upstairs. We'd agreed that I'd be better off sleeping in Samuel's bed, so that neither of us would worry about her rolling or bumping into me during the night. But whichever bed I slept in, it still required that I get up the stairs.

  At nine, Angela asked if I was ready to go to up. Since she'd gotten home, she'd been catching up on the work she'd missed that day. She worked from home for Big Brothers Big Sisters. "Before you get in anyone's bed, we need to clean that dirt and blood off of you."

  When I stepped onto the first stair step with my right leg, my weight shifted back onto my left leg. Pain ripped up, down, and around my left leg. I clutched the crutches with a white-knuckled grip and leaned to my right. I stood there with one leg on the first step and another on the first floor. When the pain decreased to a constant throb, I dragged my left leg onto the first step. I'd only have to do this fifteen more times.

Angela went around me up the stairs to pull out the cleaning and first aid supplies. I grunted my way up the stairs, sweat dripping off my forehead and my leg searing in pain. When I made it to the bathroom, Angela cleaned the dirt and dried blood off of me, applying hydrogen peroxide to the wounds that the hospital hadn't addressed. When I slid off my shorts, Angela discovered that I had two four inch long abrasions on each rear cheek. No wonder I'd found sitting somewhat painful.

I brushed my teeth, put on a clean pair of shorts and t-shirt, and then went to Samuel's room. When I lowered myself onto the bed, the room spun for a few minutes. I was growing tired of these dizzy spells every time I stood or sat. Angela followed a few minutes later with an armful of pillows. I put some under my left leg and the rest under my right arm. Even though I was exhausted, I didn't see how I'd be able to sleep that night in such an uncomfortable setup.

Angela placed my cellphone on the bedside table. "In case I can't hear you," she said and then turned off the overhead light when she left the room. I hoped that this dependence on her for every little thing wouldn't last long.

I closed my eyes, hoping that sleep would come quickly, but despite my tiredness I remained wide-awake. The entire day seemed like a wretched nightmare. I opened my eyes, closed them tight, and then re-opened them, hoping to awaken from this nightmare. Every time I opened my eyes, I saw my swollen left leg propped up on a stack of pillows. This was no dream. This was real.

I began replaying the accident, what little of it I could remember, trying to figure out this had happened. I'd looked for the cars behind me and then counted them as they passed. What had I done wrong?

Accidents happened to other people, not to me.

So why me? Why had God allowed this accident, this pain, and this trauma, to happen to me? What purpose was there in my accident? This couldn't be just some meaningless random accident. Maybe when you cut your finger, it's just a cut finger, but this accident involved major injuries, significant damages, a tremendous amount of pain, and lots of tears. There had to be a reason for it all. Nothing came to mind.

I gave up the theological debate and turned my attention to the future. The medical staff left me with a lack of confidence in their prognosis. No one, other than the EMS technician, had ever mentioned a concussion and no one had said anything to me about how long these dizzy spells might last. They hadn't even mentioned the possibility of their occurrence. How long would I be like this? Would there be any long-term ramifications? Again, answers eluded me.

Tears welled up in my eyes and as much as I tried to keep them from falling, this time they wouldn't be denied.

The entire day proved to be one of new discoveries, not a single one of them pleasant, and the night proved no different. No sooner had I fallen asleep than the nightmares started. I saw myself on my bike in the same clothes I'd worn that morning. I turned right on Pleasant Ridge, passed Martin High School, passed the entrance to the neighborhood, looked behind me, counted the cars as they passed, and then I felt the sensation of being hit in the back of the head. The sensation of being hit jolted me awake. My eyes opened wide to the darkness of the room. My heart pounded and I could feel sweat forming on my face. A few minutes later, when my heart rate returned to normal, I drifted back to sleep only to have the same nightmare and to be awakened at the point of the accident.

After three or four occurrences, I tried to fight the sleep off, fearful of the nightmare returning. I didn't want to go back to sleep. I couldn't take the nightmares anymore. I looked over at the clock and it read two-thirty. The urge to go to the bathroom pressed on me and I pushed the sheets aside and sat up. Even in the darkness, the room felt as if it were tilted and spinning at full force. Both hands grabbed a hold of the bed sheets and held on as tightly as possible while I waited for the spinning to stop.

When the spinning stopped, I pulled myself up with one of the crutches. I gasped in pain as every bone and muscle in my body hurt. The room spun again so I stood there holding onto the crutches. After that feeling passed, I shuffled into the bathroom and then back to Samuel's bedroom. I plopped down on the bed, leaned the crutch against the wall, and laid down. The room spun once more and I grabbed the bed sheets while squeezing my eyes shut.

Since my eyes were closed I didn't see Angela walk into the room. "Are you all right? I thought I heard you moving around?"

"Just had to go to the bathroom."

"How are you feeling?"

"Fine," I lied.

She went back to our room while I waited for sleep and the nightmares to return. They arrived right on schedule.

THREE
THE FIRST DAY

At some point, exhaustion wrestled the nightmares down and I slept for a few uninterrupted hours. The shining sun pierced through the east-facing window and awakened me. I blinked my eyes a few times as I tried to figure out where I was. The Pixar characters of Lightning McQueen, Sheriff Woody, and Buzz Lightyear stared down at me from the posters on the wall. I recognized the surroundings as Samuel's room, but I couldn't remember why I'd been asleep in his room. Was I dreaming? I didn't think so. I tried to recall if I'd come into Samuel's room during the night. He usually woke up once or twice and either Angela or I would have to lay down with him to get him to fall back asleep. Had last night been my turn? If so, where was Samuel?

When I reached over to get my glasses off the bedside table, all the painful memories came rushing back. My head pounded, the abrasions burned, my lower left leg throbbed, my chest hurt, and my bones and muscles ached. There wasn't a part of me that didn't hurt.

With my glasses on, I pushed myself up to a sitting position. I'd forgotten about how the room spun when I moved too quickly. I closed my eyes, which didn't help, but I kept hoping it might. When the feeling passed, I looked down at the blankets and wondered what today might hold. Would new pains develop? Would I spend the rest of the day in bed? Did I even want to venture going down the stairs since I'd have to come back up them at some point?

I looked up to see Angela standing in the doorway. "How'd you sleep?" she asked.

"Great," I lied. I kept the secret of the nightmares to myself.

"Did you want to go downstairs?" she asked.

"Maybe later."

"Did you want to take a shower?"

"Not now."

My nose appeared to be working, because something stunk and the chances were high that the stench came from me and my wounds rather than the bed or the room. But taking a shower would require too much effort.

"Would you like something to eat?"

Food sounded appealing, given that I'd eaten one meal in the last twenty-four hours. There were a number of things that I wanted, but given my physical state there were few things I thought I could eat. Cereal? I'd either spill it on me or the milk would turn the flakes disgustingly soggy given the amount of time it might take me to eat it. Eggs, waffles, pancakes, and French toast all sounded tempting, but I thought I might be pushing my luck by asking Angela to make me breakfast in bed.

"How about a peanut butter and jelly sandwich?" I proposed. I couldn't think of anything else. It wasn't exactly a breakfast staple, but it would provide me with some nutritional value and I could eat it as slowly as I wanted.

"I can do that," she replied.

While I waited, I conceded that the ER nurse had been right about one thing, I felt worse today. Still, I wasn't taking the pain reliever or the muscle relaxant. I could endure the pain.

Angela returned with a sandwich and a glass of tea. My wife knew me, I was a tea-drinker. She'd even thought ahead and put the tea in a thirty-two ounce plastic cup I'd gotten at a barbecue restaurant. This would last me an hour, maybe two.

She stepped back and stood in the doorway. Maybe she could smell me as well. "So, what are we going to do about dinner?" Angela asked.

When we were first married, Angela assumed the role of grocery shopping and cooking, even though she disliked both. She was the woman and that's what women did. After all, that's what her mother did. While she cooked, I accepted the responsibility of cleaning the kitchen, a task I despised.

Five years into our marriage, I proposed that we switch roles. At the time, we were living in a small apartment in east Arlington. We both worked fifty to sixty hours a week and Angela attended graduate school in her spare time. I arrived home one Monday night to an empty apartment, two potatoes, and some brown iceberg lettuce.

"Why don't you let me try doing the grocery shopping and cooking?" I asked her when she got home.

"No," she said. She said it in a way that indicated the matter was not up for discussion. We each ate a baked potato for dinner.

I came home the following night to an empty apartment and looked in the refrigerator to find nothing but that brown lettuce. When Angela arrived home, she looked at me and then she looked at the rotting lettuce. "Fine, you can do the shopping and the cooking."

Switching roles proved to be one of the best things we ever did in our marriage. We were both happier and there was food to eat. I didn't know much more than her about cooking when I started, but I threw myself into the task, watching cooking shows and buying cookbooks. I found that I enjoyed being in the kitchen. Eleven years later, looking at me laying in bed barely able to stand up, I'm sure the question "what will we do?" went through her mind.

I took another bite of the sandwich to stall for more time. If we ate out every meal, that might cost us about four hundred dollars a week, and that's if we ate cheaply. Forget about the health issues of eating take-out for every meal, we were in survival mode. But how long would it take us to tire of eating out, excluding Samuel? He'd love a diet of chicken nuggets, pizza, and tacos. Also, how soon would the burden of going to get every single meal wear down Angela? The other option would be for Angela to put on her cooking apron again, but I figured all of us would burn out on a menu that revolved around French toast, mac and cheese, grilled cheese sandwiches, and frozen pizzas.

I sighed. "I don't know."

"The church asked if people could bring us meals."

I knew we needed help, but I wanted to find a way to help myself rather than be dependent on other people. After all, we'd both graduated from college, so we could figure something out. We helped other people, we didn't ask for help. With enough time, I could find a solution to our food problem.

"Well?" she pressed.

My stubbornness wasn't helping the situation. If Angela had to keep watch over me, our young son, work, go to the grocery store and cook the meals, or go pick up takeout, then she might push me down the stairs to finish off what the truck driver hadn't. (I don't actually believe she would ever consider pushing me down the stairs, she's way too nice for that. The thought might cross her mind but she'd never act on it.)

"Okay, let people bring some meals."

She left to call the church back and I stayed in Samuel's bed. I thought I might pass the time reading. At first, I tried a book. I read a few pages, but couldn't remember what I'd read. I flipped back and re-read those pages, but I still didn't remember anything. I put the book aside and picked up one of the magazines Angela had purchased for me the night before, an issue of *ProCycling*. Again, I couldn't remember anything from one page to the next. I put the magazine aside as well.

I got out of bed, moving slowly to keep the dizziness at bay, and limped downstairs to the couch. I turned on the TV and watched three hours of *Law and Order*. (When I tuned in that night to watch more episodes, I found they were rerunning the ones they'd shown during the day. That ended my watching of *Law and* Order during the day.)

The pain increased as the day wore on. With the pounding headache and body aches, I wondered if I'd contracted the flu during my ER stay. A cough, sore throat, and runny nose would've convinced me completely. Still, I resisted taking anything other than the anti-inflammatories.

My cellphone vibrated with calls and texts, yet I continued to ignore them. I didn't want to talk to anyone. What was there to say? I hurt and I'm going to be hurting for quite some time. After three hours of television and with nothing else to do, I decided to check my voicemail. The first few calls were from friends wanting to make sure that I was okay and checking to see if I needed anything.

The fourth message was from an Arlington police officer. "My apologies for not getting to talk to you at the scene of the accident. Given the extent of your injuries, EMS wanted to get you to the hospital. The driver did stop, was found to be at fault, and given a ticket. There were also a couple of eyewitnesses to the accident. The driver was insured. Give me a call when you are ready and I can provide you with the pertinent information so that you can file a claim with his insurance company."

I replayed the message, scribbled down the phone number, and then called to speak with this police officer.

"Why?" the individual who answered the phone asked.

"I was in an accident yesterday. A truck hit me while I was riding a bike. This officer left me a voicemail telling me to call him so I could get the necessary information to file an insurance claim."

"The official police report won't be ready for three days. You can get it from the clerk's office then."

"The officer who left me a message said to call him at this number so I could get that information."

"Why didn't you get it at the scene?"

"Because I was hit by a truck while I was on a bicycle. I had a concussion among other injuries and EMS transported me to the ER. I never even saw the officer at the scene. He called me and told me I could call him!"

"What's the officer's name again?" he snarled.

I gave him the name.

"We have two officers by that last name. What's the first name?"

"I. Don't. Know. He didn't leave me his first name."

He let out a heavy sigh. "Male or female?"

Had he not heard me referring to the officer as a "he?" "Male," I answered.

"That officer isn't even at this station. I don't know why you called here. Hold on, while I transfer you!"

Before I was able to shoot back that the officer had given me this phone number, something I'd already told him, the line began ringing. After three rings, another person answered the phone. I explained the reason for my call again.

"Unfortunately, that officer is off duty for the next two days. I'd be happy to take your name and number and have him call you back when he returns."

I gave him my information and hung up. I didn't deserve this treatment. I'd been minding my own business, adhering to the rules and laws of the streets, when an inattentive individual hit me. The accident was not my fault, so why had this guy treated me like it was. My life, my family's life, had been flipped upside down by this accident. What about the driver? He got a ticket and went on his way. How was this fair? I clenched my left hand into a fist. I wanted to do something, scream, yell, hit something.

My cellphone vibrated. I looked at the display and saw Jeremy's name on the caller id, a friend from church. I let out a deep breath and answered the phone.

"How are you?" he asked.

"Been better," I answered and then listed the various injuries I'd suffered.

"So what happened?"

I explained that a truck had hit me while I'd been riding a bike, but because of the concussion I couldn't remember anything about the accident.

"What did the doctor say?"

"Six weeks on crutches."

"Did the driver have insurance?"

"According to the police officer, yes."

"Have you hired an attorney?"

I hesitated. "I haven't thought about that. I can't see how his insurance would be difficult about this. The guy was at fault."

"You gotta get what's coming to you."

This conversation would be repeated multiple times in the coming days with nearly every person I encountered. I began referring to this as "the spiel." When a person asked how I was doing, I started my account from just before the accident and told them everything without even waiting for them to ask a question.

"What time can we bring dinner over? Shawna made lasagna and chocolate chip cookies."

"Six or so should be fine."

Homemade chocolate chip cookies? Those were my number one favorite food to eat. Maybe it wouldn't be so bad having people bring us meals.

"Okay, we'll see you around six. One more question, have you got plenty of Tylenol?"

"I'm good."

I put the phone next to me on the couch. Why had Jeremy asked me if I had enough Tylenol? Why Tylenol? Tylenol? Acetaminophen? I wondered if I could take Tylenol to give me relief from these aches and pains, from this headache. I knew aspirin was out because it would cause an adverse reaction with the anti-inflammatory, but I hadn't thought about Tylenol. Not trusting my brain, I googled Tylenol to see if there would be a bad reaction with the anti-inflammatory I was taking. I couldn't find any. Next, I googled Oxycodone, more out of curiosity than temptation, and discovered that a portion of it consisted of acetaminophen. Tylenol! I grabbed the crutches and stood up, stopped, waited for the room to stop spinning, and then I shuffled into the kitchen. I found a bottle of Tylenol and tossed a couple of pills down the back of my throat. Ten minutes later, the aches and pains had dissipated.

    As one problem would be alleviated, perhaps even modified through the use of over the counter medications, another would arise to take its place. A few minutes before six, the doorbell rang. Jeremy was early and I salivated in anticipation of a batch of homemade chocolate chip cookies. Maybe I could sneak one or two before dinner. Angela and Samuel answered the door while I stayed seated on the couch.

    Instead of Jeremy and his family, another couple from church, Paul and Velda, stood at the door with a meal for us. Angela led Velda to the kitchen with dinner while Paul sat on the couch to my right. I started going through "the spiel." When Velda finished in the kitchen, she came and sat on a chair to my left. We moved onto other topics, realizing that not only had we both lived in San Antonio, but we'd also lived blocks from one another. As I turned my head from the left to the right to look at each of them when they asked a question, I became dizzy. Then while Paul talked, I discovered that if I looked directly at him, my head would start hurting and my field of vision would begin to narrow. What was happening? I kept nodding my head as he talked, hoping that they couldn't tell something was wrong with me. I found that when I looked at a spot just above Paul's head, my vision would improve.

    The doorbell rang again and this time Jeremy and his daughter, Emerson, walked in with lasagna and chocolate chip cookies. After they put their meal on the kitchen counter, Jeremy sat in a chair directly in front of me. I looked straight ahead at him rather than continuing to turn my head from side to side. Emerson, a year younger than Samuel, walked right up to me and looked at the injuries on my face, staring at the cuts and abrasions as if she were trying to memorize each one of them.

"Emerson," Jeremy scolded.

"It's fine. I don't mind," I said, as she continued looking at my injuries.

Both families left after a few minutes. While Angela and Samuel escorted them to the front door, I leaned back against the couch, more tired and exhausted from that fifteen minute conversation than if I'd ridden sixty miles on a bike.

We ate dinner and I enjoyed a half dozen of the chocolate chip cookies. Finally, a perk to my injuries. I returned to the couch and watched TV while Angela put Samuel to bed. She returned to her office and kept working, still catching up from our day in the ER.

At nine p.m., the doorbell rang.

I sighed. "Who could that be?"

More people from church? Maybe some people had decided to stop by after Wednesday night church. Or another friend? Someone else with food? Whoever it was, I hoped they wouldn't stay long.

Angela peeked through one of the front windows. "It's Officer Bill."

Bill lived directly behind us and worked as a sergeant with the Arlington Police Department. We'd nicknamed him "Officer Bill." From time to time, he and I talked over the fence and a few weeks before Samuel and I had gone swimming at his house.

He sat down on the couch to my left. "I was on duty when the report of the accident came in. I tried to notify Angela, but someone had already called her. How are you?"

I gave him "the spiel."

"Have you spoken with the officer at the scene yet?"

"No, when I called, they said he was off for today and tomorrow."

"I'll tell you what I know. The driver drove a white Ford Ranger pickup truck. He did not appear to be under the influence of anything and he claimed not to have been texting or making a phone call at the time of the accident. He said he didn't see you until he hit you. The impact broke off the side view mirror of his truck. The car behind him witnessed the entire accident and called 911. The witnesses said you were doing everything right."

I tried to find consolation in that, but doing everything right hadn't prevented the accident and it wouldn't erase these injuries or the pain.

"By the way, the guy was driving his company truck. He works for Dr. Pepper."

With those words, I felt a huge burden lifted off my shoulders. Not only did the driver have insurance, he had company insurance, Fortune 500 company insurance. At last, some good news.

FOUR
THE FIRST WEEK

In addition to warning of the impending pain I would be feeling the day following the accident, that same ER nurse had advised me to "follow up with your primary care physician." Since I continued to experience new symptoms, my confidence waned in the diagnosis and prognosis of my injuries by the ER staff. No one, aside from the EMS technician, ever mentioned that I might've had a concussion or what side effects I might experience from my head trauma. They failed to treat and clean a number of my cuts and abrasions. If I hadn't nearly collapsed while trying to walk to the bathroom, they might've sent me home without crutches.

On Thursday morning, I woke up in Samuel's bed again, swallowed a couple of Tylenol, and before doing anything else, I called two doctors, Dr. Andrews, my primary care physician, and Dr. M, my trusted orthopedist. The earliest appointment I could get with Dr. Andrews was for the following Tuesday. Given the severity of my injuries, I'd hoped for an earlier appointment, but I took it anyway.

Next, I called Dr. M's office.

"Have you been to see the doctor before?" the receptionist asked.

Had I? In 2005, for a separated shoulder. In 2007, for a swollen right knee. And earlier that year for tendonitis in the left knee.

"Yes, I have."

"Why do you need to see the doctor?"

I gave her a condensed version of "the spiel."

"What's a divot fracture?"

She's just the receptionist I reminded myself. Besides, until suffering this particular fracture myself, I hadn't known what a divot fracture was. I explained it as best I could.

"I'll have to check with the doctor and get back to you. Can I have your number?"

Get back to me? Why would she need to check with the doctor to set an appointment?

Maybe she needed to check with him to see if he could fit me in that day. The accident I described did sound horrific. I gave her my cellphone number.

I sat upright in Samuel's bed waiting for the Tylenol to take affect. Angela brought me a peanut butter and jelly sandwich along with a glass of iced tea.

"I thought I heard you talking on the phone and figured you might be hungry."

"Thanks. What do you think about hiring an attorney?"

"I don't know."

The relief of learning that Dr. Pepper would be financially responsible for the accident turned to worry over night. At first, I thought that a global company would want to avoid any negative publicity and therefore do the right thing. But what if they didn't? What if they tried to cheat me? What if they turned this into a drawn out battle? In a normal mental state, I might've been able to combat their insurance adjustor, but my brain had been rattled by this accident. There were the constant headaches, the inability to concentrate, things I hadn't mentioned to Angela yet. Anyone might be able to take advantage of me in my mental state.

Despite the advice of friends, "Soak 'em for every penny," and "Congratulations on winning the lottery," I didn't see this accident as a means, or even the means, to upgrade my lifestyle, quadruple my net worth, or secure my retirement. We wanted the medical bills paid, the bike replaced (I'm not sure how Angela felt about that), and a little something for our mental anguish.

"This seems like it might be a little beyond us," I said.

"Yeah, let's get an attorney."

I looked at her and she stared right back at me.

"So, who do I call?"

Angela shrugged her shoulders.

Prior to going to work as a pastor at a church, I worked for an investment firm, Fortune Financial Services, for nearly ten years. In that time, I'd met plenty of attorneys, but they specialized in either business planning, estate planning, or divorce. I couldn't remember ever meeting a personal injury attorney while I worked there. I considered the lawyer who'd drawn up our wills and powers of attorney, but I hadn't spoken to him in five or six years. He never mentioned handling any personal injury cases either. I remembered a lawyer friend from a previous church we attended. I knew he took these types of cases because he'd told me about a case or two that he'd handled. But, when Angela and I started attending another church, this friend and I didn't part on the best of terms. Although we never exchanged harsh words, we disagreed on the way some staff members, close friends of mine, were dismissed.

Angela returned to her office to work while I tried to think of an attorney, or even a friend that might know of an attorney, that I could call. Most of the people I knew from college had become ministers or teachers rather than lawyers. As for people from my high school, I'd only kept up with one friend and he sold cars for a living. I scrolled through the contacts on my phone until I saw Mick's name. Mick! Of course. He was an attorney who attended church with us. How could I have forgotten about Mick? I'd even been to his office and gone to lunch with him. This lapse further demonstrated to me that my brain wasn't functioning normally. I couldn't remember what he'd told me about his area of specialization but I figured he could direct me to someone trustworthy who handled personal injury cases.

I called his office and the receptionist put me through to him. "Hey, Mick, I don't know if you've heard about my accident."

He had. Joe had sent an email to the entire church.

"Here's why I'm calling. The guy who hit me works for Dr. Pepper and was driving a company truck. I think I need an attorney who can help me with this."

"Hold on, let me grab a pad and take some notes."

When he came back, he reminded me that he handled personal injury cases.

"You're hired," I said.

We went over the accident, what little of it I could remember, my day at the ER, and my condition since then. He peppered me with questions and then he said, "Write everything down. What hurts, what you feel, your expenses, anything and everything."

I made notes on a piece of paper. Being right handed and my right arm being covered in an arm length abrasion, my writing looked more awful than normal. I hoped I could read it later.

"Here's why," he continued, "in a few weeks, when you are feeling better, you might downplay how bad you actually felt. If we have to go to trial, which we might, you never know how these cases will turn out, you want to have documented everything that you have been through. Your memory could be fuzzy or you could get confused."

I wrote the words "document all."

"And then, take pictures of everything. Every single injury. The property damage. All of it."

I wrote "pictures."

"Getting better is your number one priority. I'll handle the rest."

While eating leftover lasagna for lunch, we decided to go to the fire station to pick up my bike. I suggested the idea. Having been secluded in the house for a day and a half, I wanted to look at something other than the walls of our home. I also wanted to see the damage that this guy had inflicted on the bike. I strapped the bike rack to the trunk of Angela's car and that little effort caused me to breakout in a downpour of sweat. When I finished, I leaned against the car, worn out from the effort.

We drove five minutes to the station and Angela parked to the right of the building out of the path of the fire trucks and ambulances. A few firemen saw us approaching and they offered to give Samuel a tour. Angela went with Samuel while I walked with one of the firefighters who'd offered to carry my bike to the car.

"Sure glad to see you're okay," he said.

I guessed that he must've been on duty the morning of my accident, but I couldn't remember anyone from that morning. I thought about asking him about the accident, but I didn't want to know. Besides, he only had knowledge of what happened after the accident. He leaned the bike against the car and offered to put it on the rack for me.

"I got it. Thanks," I said.

I leaned my crutches against the car and grabbed my bike to wheel it towards me. It wouldn't roll, which explained why the firefighter had carried it. I stepped closer to the bike to inspect the damage. Both wheels had been bent to such an extent that they couldn't roll more than a few inches without getting stuck in the forks. Those could be repaired, I thought. Just a little truing of the wheel and maybe some new spokes. I reached down to pick up the bike by the handlebars and realized that a portion of the handlebars was missing. The drops on the left side, the part below the brake and gear shifter, were gone. This must've been where his side view mirror smacked into the bike. The force and speed of the impact must've sheared off that part of the handlebars. Fortunately, my hands hadn't been there. Normally, I rode bent over with my hands in the drops. If they had been there, instead of on top of the handlebars, his side view mirror would've hit the back of my arm rather than the handlebars.

I checked out the rest of the bike. Both shifters were broken. There were tire marks across a part of frame. With my finger, I pressed on that spot of the carbon fiber frame and could feel the frame give when I touched it. He'd cracked the frame when he ran over the bike. I realized how "lucky" I'd been. If I'd been a few inches that way or this way, then I could've been seriously impaired or killed. I didn't know what had happened when he'd hit me, but I guessed that I'd been tossed in the air. If I'd been tossed in a different direction, he could've run over me like he had the bike.

I took a deep breath and put the bike on the rack. While I waited for Samuel to finish his fire station tour, I kept my back to the bike, unable to look at its mangled mess and be reminded of what could've happened.

"How is it?" Angela asked when we got in the car.

"Destroyed." I didn't mention that he'd cracked the frame by running over it or that he'd sheared off a portion of the handlebars.

The receptionist from Dr. M's office didn't call me back on Thursday, so I called them again on Friday morning. This time I spoke with a different receptionist and we went through the whole thing again, my accident, my prior relationship with the doctor, and what a divot fracture was.

"I called and spoke with someone yesterday. They said they would call me back, but never did."

"Do you know who you spoke to?"

"Um. I don't remember her name."

"That's no problem. Can you hold for a moment?"

"Sure."

I listened to the hold music. I hoped that the receptionist from the previous day wouldn't get into any trouble. She'd probably gotten busy and forgotten to call me back. Or Dr. M never gave her an answer. Either way, no problem.

"Mr. Dikes, can I have your number so we can call you back?"

"Um, I guess so."

Why couldn't they make me an appointment? What was so difficult about that? I could feel my pulse rising. Calm down, I told myself. Your accident and injuries sound horrific. She's trying to get you an appointment for that day. I made these assumptions without asking her. I gave her my cellphone number but I also made sure to ask for her name.

"Cathy," she said.

Mick came by our house on Friday afternoon. He was a short, Italian guy in his mid-fifties who still spoke with a bit of a Chicago accent, where he'd been born and raised. His wife, Vivian, had sent along a giant platter of spaghetti for us. Samuel loved eating her spaghetti. We discussed the accident, the ER, and the injuries again. Then I signed a form authorizing him to act on my behalf. When we finished reviewing the accident, he asked if I'd be willing to take him to the scene of the accident.

"Sure. I'm not sure exactly where it happened, but I have a general idea."

We got in his car and drove around the corner to Pleasant Ridge.

"The last thing I remembering is passing the entrance to my neighborhood. The accident happened after that somewhere along here."

We looked for some sign that my accident had occurred on Tuesday, but there was nothing. No tire marks. Not even a pool of dried blood indicating where I'd landed. A person wouldn't even be able to tell that an accident had taken place here.

Mick parked the car and got out to take a few pictures. I stayed seated. He took pictures from both directions, from where the driver came from and the direction he would've been going. When he finished, he took me home. "Get better," he reminded me.

Everyone kept saying that to me, but they weren't in my position. They weren't feeling my pain, not knowing when it would stop hurting and start to feel better.

I walked inside and checked the time. It was ten after five. Once more, Dr. M's office had failed to call me back. Why? What was the problem? What had I done to deserve this treatment? I arrived early for my appointments, treated the staff with respect, and paid my bill on time. I even referred other people to his office. Why were they refusing to call me back?

I didn't want to go back to the orthopedist from JPS. Besides the fact that he didn't take my insurance, his abrupt manner in the ER had turned me off. Maybe I could ask Dr. Andrews for a recommendation, but I wanted to see Dr. M. I'd been to his office for three separate injuries and each time he'd helped me get back on the bike. I valued his expertise.

I returned to my spot on the couch and turned on the TV.

On Saturday, I remembered that a friend from church, Bill, knew Dr. M. I thought that he might be able to help me bypass the office staff. But I didn't have Bill's phone number.

As for the church, I'd been given a temporary leave of absence from work. "Come back when you're ready," I was told, "but if you can make it to one of the Sunday services, that'd be great."

Since I was quickly tiring of being in the house all the time, I decided to go to church on Sunday morning. I also hoped to see Bill. When we arrived, I found that some people hadn't heard about the accident, so they were shocked to see me walk into church on crutches with gauze covering my right arm and stitches on my face. I gave a condensed version of "the spiel" while I kept an eye out for Bill. When I saw him walk in, I made my way over to him and explained my predicament. "Can you help me get an appointment?"

"I'll call him right after church. Text me your number so I can text you back."

I texted him right then.

Thirty minutes after church Bill texted me. "Call in the a.m. Give them my name. The doctor has another doctor on staff. He'll get you in."

I called Dr. M's office on Monday morning, spoke with a receptionist, and passed along the message that Bill had given me.

"Can I put you on hold for a moment?" the receptionist asked.

I assured myself that she just needed to verify my story with Dr. M and then figure out when she could fit me in. I listened to the hold music and waited.

"Mr. Dikes, can I have a number where I can call you back?"

WHAT?!?!?! What?! What had I done? Could somebody please tell me what I'd done to get blacklisted by his office? Whatever I'd done, they must have me confused with someone else. I took another deep breath and composed myself. One more chance. If they didn't call me back that day, I'd find another orthopedist. I gave my phone number to a receptionist for the third time.

An hour later she called me back to setup an appointment.

FIVE
THIS IS LUCKY?

I grew tired of talking about the accident. Every time I answered the door or phone, people wanted to know about it. My inbox was flooded with people emailing me. People I hadn't spoken with in years called to check on me. At least with emails, I could copy and paste the details from a previous email but phone calls required effort and interaction. Before the accident, I might go a week without bumping into someone in public. Now, no matter where I went I kept intersecting with people I hadn't seen in months. Every time I went somewhere, people, even total strangers, wanted to know what had happened. I wanted to step out of my skin and mind and come back when I'd returned to normal. But when would that be? Barely a week had passed. I couldn't take much more of this. The physical pain had diminished, but the mental and emotional burden only grew worse.

Dr. M's receptionist set me an appointment for Monday afternoon to see Dr. Shane, a new doctor in their office. He was about six feet tall, broad shouldered and athletic looking. And he wore a suit. Not many people still wore a suit in August in Texas. He ordered x-rays and after he'd looked at them, he asked me to lie back on the examination table. "Let's take a look at all of your injuries," he said.

He proceeded to push, pull, twist, and turn both legs and arms. Then, he instructed me to sit up and push against his hands with my fists. After that, he rotated my thumbs in every direction. "I want to take a look at your arm," he said as he removed the gauze that I'd wrapped around my entire right arm.

"You were very lucky," Dr. Shane said after he'd rewrapped my arm.

I'd heard that before. I was tired of hearing that.

"I'm going to put you in a walking boot for the fracture. This'll protect your leg from anyone bumping into it and further injuring that bone. Keep using the crutches for a few more days."

I braced myself for the rest of his prognosis, expecting that he would tell how I might not be able to ride a bike or run or that the rehabilitation would be long and lengthy.

"Take it easy and come back in three weeks or so. You're going to heal up very nicely." He smiled, shook my hand, and left the room. A nurse entered the room a few minutes later and fitted me with a walking boot.

I walked out of the office to the car and put the crutches in the back seat. Even though he'd advised me to use them for a few more days, I was done with those things. They pressed into an area of my chest that hurt and every step compounded that pain.

Two days later, I sat on the examination table of Dr. Andrew's office. We were about the same age and she had a son a year older than mine. On a previous visit, she'd guessed that I was a cyclist.

"How'd you know?" I asked.

"Shaved legs and a clearly defined tan line at the midpoint of your thigh means there's a ninety-nine point nine percent chance that you're a cyclist."

This morning, she sat on a stool across from me and asked about what injuries I'd incurred besides the broken bone.

"They mentioned a possible concussion."

They being the EMS technician and not the ER doctor.

"Having dizziness and headaches?"

"Yes."

"Getting worse or diminishing?"
"Diminishing somewhat."
The dizziness was. Instead of making its presence known every time I stood up, it struck me periodically and unexpectedly. The daily headaches continued, albeit less intense than they'd been the first few days.
"They should go away eventually, but if they don't then call me back."
She got up from her chair and removed the gauze and bandaging from my right arm. "Changing the bandages and cleaning the abrasions?"
"Daily."
"Good. I think your arm will heal up just fine. I'll have the nurse wrap your arm again." She paused and wrote notes in my file. "Seen an orthopedist?"
"Yes."
She stopped writing in my file and looked directly at me. "You know, you were very lucky."
Those words again.
People kept telling me this and for a guy who was supposed to be so very lucky, I didn't feel that way. I lived with a constant headache and gulped Tylenol four times a day, first thing in the morning, then late morning, late afternoon, and the last thing before I went to bed. My left thumb remained swollen and achy, lacking the strength to open a bag of chips or even a Clif Bar. Every time I walked by a mirror, I saw the cuts, the scratches, the bruises, and the abrasions. After a few nights, I'd gone back to the bed in our room, but deep, refreshing sleep eluded me. Between the nightmares, keeping my left leg and right arm elevated to reduce their swelling, I barely slept at night. I was tired and grouchy.
And then there was the daily changing of the bandaging on my right arm. I removed the gauze, which I sometimes had to rewrap two or three times a day when it came loose. After the gauze came off, I peeled away the non-stick bandages. Most days, they lived up to their

advertising as being non-stick, but sometimes they'd peel off a sliver of skin. When I finished removing everything, I saw a messy mixture of blood and puss that showed no signs of improvement. It looked the same every day. I reapplied the white cream of silver sulfadiazine cream, gingerly applied three new non-stick bandages, and rolled my arm in new white gauze.

Prior to the accident, I dealt with stress by going on a two or three hour bike ride. If I were crunched for time, maybe a one hour ride. In desperate situations, I headed off to the gym to spin away on a stationary bike or run on the treadmill. The physical activity helped release the tension. But in my present condition, the stress swelled within me.

I couldn't do much of anything, not even get on the floor and play with Samuel. The only things I could do were sit on the couch and eat. People continued bringing us food and with every delivery came a new batch of sweets. I guess they figured it would make me feel better and to an extent they were right. I ate pies, cakes, cookies, and brownies. Prior to the accident, I might have indulged in a dessert once or twice a week, but now I binged at least twice a day.

Dr. Shane told me that I could remove the walking boot at home. "But be careful," he warned.

At night, I sat on the couch and removed my leg from the constraints of the boot and peeled off a sock that had simmered in sweat the entire day. Samuel snatched the boot away from me, strapping it to his leg and hobbling around the house.

"Look, I'm Daddy."

When he finished playing with my walking boot, he kept it with him on the other side of the house. Maybe he thought I couldn't walk without it and I wouldn't be able to come get it. Even my son could sense the stress building within me.

My experience with injuries healing in a timely manner had been mixed, which combined with my increasingly pessimistic outlook, led me to worry that my divot fracture wouldn't heal on schedule. At fifteen, I broke my right arm in two places a few inches from my wrist. When they discharged me from the hospital a week later in a cast that extended from my shoulder to the tips of my fingers, the doctor told me I'd be in a cast for six weeks. "Six weeks tops," were his precise words. When I returned to his office on the appointed date, he took one look at the x-rays and confined me to the cast for an additional three weeks. "The bones haven't sufficiently melded together." Three weeks later, the bones still hadn't healed to his satisfaction, but he did remove the portion of the cast that extended from my elbow to the shoulder. He didn't even bother to predict when I might be free from the rest of the plaster. "Come back in three weeks and we'll see." It was then, twelve weeks after the injury, six weeks after his initial prognostication, that he removed the cast.

Earlier in 2009, I'd visited Dr. M when I'd experienced a sharp pain just above my left knee. The pain began the day after I'd participated in a ninety-five mile bike ride, ninety of those miles going into a twenty-five mile an hour headwind. I took a few days off the bike but every time I tried to ride, the pain came back. I described it to him as a "sharp, cutting sensation just above the kneecap."

"Tendonitis," he declared. "With rest and physical therapy, you should be good to go in two to three weeks."

It ended up being ten weeks.

So I hoped that this time the news would be better. I didn't want to hear "Your leg needs more time to heal" or the draconian declaration of "Your leg isn't healing properly. We'll need to operate."

The best part about having a broken bone, if there can be a best part, is that pain lasts for about a week. This had been the fourth time I'd broken a bone and every time the pain went away within seven days. The worst part was the fact that the lack of pain gave no indication as to whether or not the bone had actually healed.

I tried to be positive and focus on what the recovery process might look like when Dr. Shane freed me from this walking boot. Physical therapy? Walking? Light jogging? Strength training? Work on the stationary bike? And then how long would that last?

More often than not, attempts to think positive lasted only briefly. "I'm never going to get better," or "It's going to take forever for me to get better."

The diminishing pain and lack of activity left me with ample time to dwell on the question of why this had happened to me. What had I done to deserve this?

When I could push these questions aside, people brought them back to me. It was as if they were saying to me "You are a pastor, so there must be a reason this occurred to you. Share that reason with us so the same thing doesn't happen to us." Maybe they thought I was someone who ought to know God better or that I had a direct line to God. If they could figure out why I had suffered this ordeal, then they might be able to escape or even endure their own particular trials. Some even hinted that a sovereign God allowed things, even instigated things, to bring about change in our lives. The subtext of their words being that I must be engaged in some secret sin, have some unrepentant sin, or be Jonah-like in refusing to go in the direction God was leading me. These few, although they wouldn't accuse me directly, hinted that God might have removed His hand from me to discipline me. Others suggested that God allowed me to experience such an accident so that I might be an example to others in the church. "The way you handle this will help others handle their own problems." A few hinted that I might be in for a Job-like season of life. "Be prepared for things to get worse." And I think, in their own way, each person was trying to help me, but I could've done without their help.

Someone even suggested that bike riding had become too important to me. "Maybe God wants you to spend more time with your family. You do seem to ride your bike quite a

70

lot." Oh yes, somebody did say that to me. With a straight face. Without even a hint of a smile on their face.

To each and all of these, I politely nodded my head and said "Maybe," if I said anything at all. Everyone had an opinion as to what God wanted to tell me, if He even wanted to tell me anything. As for the assertion that God wanted to get my attention for riding my bike too much, I'm certain that if Angela and Samuel could've figured out a way to strap me to a bike where I could pedal safely with one leg and burn off a little tension, they would've gladly, even quickly, purchased such a device.

God never told me about an unrepentant sin from my past or exposed a sin I didn't know about or alerted me to the direction in life I was supposed to go but was too busy to hear or any other such stuff. Maybe He does use those sorts of circumstances to speak into other people's lives. I was open to hearing the rationale for my accident, but I never heard anything.

That doesn't mean I didn't ask repeatedly.

Sometimes, we never figure out "why." Maybe the answer is learning to live with the tension of the unknown. The Bible contains accounts of people who suffered more than I did and many of them never had the question of why answered. Instead, they endured.

Some suggested that God was attempting to get the attention of the driver. That's great, but my only question would be why God didn't have him run into a pole instead of a human being. I don't know what happened to the driver. I never heard a word from him.

I might've learned one thing. When people are hurting and in pain, when they are in the depths of the valley, instead of answers and solutions, maybe they need someone who will sit next to them quietly. Perhaps they need someone who will look them in the eye and listen to them in their noise and in their silence.

  I needed something to shift my focus from the constant negativity of the accident. The obstacles seemed overwhelming, pain was a constant companion, the medical bills were piling up, and I hated that walking boot. Perhaps, I thought, I needed to start thinking about what life would be like when I was better. Maybe if I focused on a particular goal, my mind wouldn't dwell on the other aspects of my recovery. The goal needed to be audacious as well as desirable. I could think of only one thing. After the nightmares had stopped recurring, about ten days after the accident, I began to consider riding a bike again. It was something that I loved that I wanted to do again. What if I bought a new bike now? Maybe seeing a new bike in the garage every day would give me a sense of hope as well as purpose.

  This was a great idea. But there was just one problem. How was I going to buy a bike while my leg was still in a walking boot? Before purchasing a bike, I'd want to test ride it. How could I do that or get around that? And then there was the matter of paying for the bike. The purchase would run into the thousands of dollars. Money I didn't have at the moment. Until I received a clean bill of health from Dr. Shane, Mick couldn't initiate settlement talks with Dr. Pepper.

  Despite the flaws in my plan, I proceeded. I'd figure something out when I got to the bike shop. Besides, I knew what I needed and wanted. My previous two bikes had been manufactured by Trek so I planned on sticking with them. Road bikes come in different frame sizes and both of mine had been sixties, so I knew the size I needed. Armed with that information, I thought that I could buy the bike I wanted and make any other adjustments when Dr. Shane cleared me to ride again. Just seeing the bike would be motivation enough for me.

  I went to a bike shop near my house and wandered up and down the aisles, looking for a carbon fiber Trek road bike in my size. They didn't have any. I lingered in the aisles, hoping that an employee might talk to me, but in the twenty minutes I stood there not a single one of them approached me.

One of the perks of living in the Dallas-Fort Worth area is the plethora of bike shops. I left this one and drove to another one ten minutes away. I found a number of models that intrigued me, but once more there was nothing in the size I needed. Again, the employees avoided me, even when I parked myself in front of the most expensive bike in the shop. It was as if I didn't even exist. They walked right past me without saying a word.

I drove thirty minutes away to a third bike shop, hoping for a different outcome, but the results were the same.

So much for optimism. I drove home in silence, not even bothering to turn on the radio. This was a sign about my health and future. Being ignored by the employees of three different bike shops had nothing to do with me being in a walking boot, but everything to do with the fact that my leg wasn't healed. That's what my Sunday afternoon meant. My follow up appointment with Dr. Shane was a few days away, but I already knew what he'd say, "The leg hasn't healed." I wouldn't be doing anything anytime soon.

I arrived at Dr. Shane's office on a Wednesday morning. His nurse escorted me back to an examination room and then the radiology technician retrieved me to take x-rays of my leg. On my first visit, he'd been talkative asking me questions about the accident. He'd even showed me the x-rays of my leg, pointing out where the divot was. On this visit, he spoke only to give me directions as to how and where to place my leg. When he finished, he took me back to the examination room without even showing me the x-rays.

This was not good.

The paper crinkled underneath me as I fidgeted from side to side. On the wall, I saw autographed pictures of professional athletes who'd been patients of Dr. M and Dr.

Shane. "Thanks for getting be back on the field," or "You're the best!" A computer hummed on the desk across from me. Dr. M had gone digital so instead of printing the x-rays they were stored on the computer network. I wondered if I could locate them easily and look at them myself. But what if Dr. Shane caught me? What if I accidentally deleted a file?

I sat there debating what to do for ten minutes. Then, there was a knock on the door and Dr. Shane entered the room. Again, he wore a suit. "How are you?" he asked.

"Better, I hope."

He sat down on a stool in front of the computer and pulled up the file with my x-rays. His head was directly in front of the screen making it impossible for me to see the pictures. I moved to the right but still couldn't make anything out so I slid to the left and was able to see the pictures of my leg. The divot was still there. My leg hadn't healed. I knew it. I turned away and looked at the wall while Dr. Shane continued looking at the x-rays. Maybe he was perplexed by the lack of healing in my bone and didn't know what to say.

He shut off the screen and stood up. "Lay back on the table," he said and then he evaluated my leg as he had before, pushing, pulling, twisting, and turning it. The only difference this time being that it didn't hurt. Also like last time, Dr. Shane asked me to make a fist and push against his hands.

"Have a seat," he said when he'd finished his examination.

My back and neck stiffened. I clenched my jaw as I awaited the news, the bad news.

"Other than some scar tissue, you appear fine. The x-ray looks clean."

I was confused. I thought I'd seen a divot on the x-ray. "So my leg has healed?"

"Yeah. I compared the old x-rays with the new. The bone has completely healed."

"Great." I paused and waited for him to continue, but he didn't say anything. "So now what?"

"Continue to wear the boot when you're around crowds. We wouldn't want anyone to fall into you and re-injure your leg."

He paused and I waited for him to prescribe physical therapy or set some parameters for my workouts, but he didn't add anything else. "When can I resume my activities? Biking? Running?"

"I don't see any reason to wait. Be careful, listen to your body, and don't get hit by anymore trucks." He chuckled at his joke.

I didn't.

"So, no physical therapy?"

"Nah, you'll be fine."

"What about the other injuries? The continued soreness in my chest and thumb?"

"Those'll take time. You have deep bruises, but in a few months, you should be fine." He reached out and shook my hand. "Call me if you have any problems." Then he turned and left the room.

I followed him out and stopped at the receptionist's desk to pay my bill. Four weeks and a day had passed since the accident and now I was free to resume my life from before the accident.

If only it were that easy.

SIX
FORWARD OR BACKWARD?

Now that I'd gotten my clearance from Dr. Shane, I could move on with my life. Although he'd recommended that I continue to wear the walking boot for a few weeks as a precaution, I took it off as soon as I got to the car and tossed it into the trunk. I was done with that bulky thing.

The next step would be to get on a bike again, which left me with the task of buying a bike with money I didn't have. When I called Mick to tell him that I'd been a given medical clearance, he told me that we needed to wait for all the medical bills to arrive. Then he could initiate settlement talks with Dr. Pepper.

I had no money but I wanted and needed a bike. I hadn't figured out a way around the money issue, but I decided to go bike shopping anyway. I usually had Thursday afternoons off from the church so I blocked out the entire afternoon for visiting another bike shop.

The night before, with the excitement of shopping for a new bike filling my mind, I tossed and turned until a little after midnight. When I finally fell asleep, the nightmares I thought had left me, the ones that haunted me for ten days after the accident, returned in full force. The nightmare was the same as it had been before with me riding on Pleasant Ridge and then the sensation of being struck in the back of the head. At the point of impact in the dream, I woke up to a racing heartbeat and a face full of sweat. I took a few deep breaths to calm down, fell back asleep, and was jolted awake by the same nightmare. The pattern continued throughout the night.

After the fourth or fifth time, I tried to reason with my frightened self. This was a freak accident, a million to one chance. There was nothing to fear.

But, the other part of me countered, the next time I got hit I might not be as lucky. I should be responsible and think about Angela and Samuel. How would they be affected if I were paralyzed or even killed?

So I should be afraid? Take up running? While I'd been recuperating, there were news reports of two different runners being struck by cars. Safety was not guaranteed. Besides, I'd ridden thousands of miles over the years and never been hit.

The arguments went back and forth in my mind. By morning, I wasn't sure I wanted to ride a bike again. Fear had entered the picture. Not of riding, but of what might happen. The practical side of me wondered about spending thousands of dollars on a new bike. What if I spent that money, but couldn't persuade myself to get on it? Shouldn't I wait to see if these fears went away before I made such a purchase?

Since I didn't have the money to spend, I decided to just look at what I might buy.

After a morning of work, I got in my car and drove an hour to Richardson Bike Mart, one of the largest bike shops in the area. I'd frequented this store when I worked for Fortune Financial Services. Their office was ten minutes away from Richardson Bike Mart.

I arrived and headed straight for the road bikes, walking past a group of employees, none of whom offered to help me. I walked up and down the aisles looking at the various bikes but not finding anything in my size or to my liking. I stood in front of one bike, wondering why I couldn't catch the attention of a single employee. There was no walking boot to ward them off. Did I look like a guy who didn't have the money to spend? My growling stomach reminded me that I'd skipped lunch to drive to Richardson. I checked my phone to see if I could find a nearby bike shop to stop at on the way home.

"Can I help you?"

I glanced up, expecting to see this voice talking to someone near me. Instead, I saw a stocky guy with blond hair and glasses standing next to me. He was wearing cargo shorts and a blue pullover with the Richardson Bike Mart logo on the front.

"Oh yeah," I said as I put my phone away.

"I'm Glynn," he said, "What can I do for you?"

"I need a new road bike," I began and then I gave him "the spiel." "I want a bike similar to what I had, a Trek Madone, and I need a size sixty. I can't seem to find anything like that here."

Glynn nodded his head.

"And I'm just looking today. I haven't settled with Dr. Pepper yet so I don't have the money to buy anything."

"Are you sure?"

I was confused. "About what?"

"I'd think you'd need something smaller than a sixty. You look like a fifty-eight would fit you better."

"Well, my previous two bikes were sixties."

Great. Someone finally came over to help me and he had no clue what he was talking about. Two other bike shops had sized me when I purchased bikes and those guys had concluded, independently of one another, that a sixty centimeter frame would be best for me. I knew what I needed.

"We can measure you, but just from looking at you, I think you'd be more comfortable in a fifty-eight. I would think that a sixty would give you neck and shoulder issues."

"I tried a fifty-eight before and it didn't feel right." I'd done so when I bought my second bike. I tried it not for a better fit but because the store had knocked a thousand dollars off the sticker price. But I did have trouble with my neck and shoulder. The day before the accident I'd made an appointment to be re-fitted on my bike because of those problems. Maybe a different size bike would help. I hadn't planned on a complete re-evaluation of my bike setup.

"How about this? Let's put two bikes on a turbo trainer, a fifty-eight and a sixty, let you spin for awhile, and see which one feels better."

That made sense, and it wasn't as if I had anything else to do that day.

He rolled two Trek road bikes back to the fitting area where three turbo trainers were lined up, none of them being used at the moment. He slid the back wheel axle into the trainer and then placed the front wheel into a riser block, which would prevent the bike from tipping over while I pedaled. While he set the bikes up, Glynn told me dozens of stories of other accidents, none of which I found comforting. I asked about his family to change the subject and discovered that we each had one child, the differences being his daughter was a teenager and my son was three.

He beamed with pride when he spoke about his daughter who'd won an academic scholarship to The Oakridge School, a private prep school. "I made a deal with her. If she gets a full academic scholarship to college, I'll buy her whatever car she wants. Last week, she gave me a BMW car catalog. I may have to amend our deal," he said with a laugh. He pointed me to the first bike he'd set up. "This is a sixty, just like you had. Hop on and start pedaling whenever you're ready."

I swung my right leg over the frame, sat down on the seat, and started to pedal. I began slowly. I hadn't been on a bike or engaged in any physical activity in four weeks. My left leg, particularly the calf, ached and hurt from the muscles being stretched for the first time since the accident. Every downturn of the pedal felt like a muscle spasm.

"How do you feel?"

"Not bad," I grunted. I clenched my jaw, as if that might help me push the pain back down. "This feels similar to my old bike."

"Well, you look really stretched out and uncomfortable." He unwound an odd-shaped ruler and measured the angle of my shoulder extension. "You're way out of the recommended alignment."

I took his word for this, although I had no idea what it meant. "This is how I always felt. I thought this was normal."

"Let's get you on the other bike."

I switched bikes and started pedaling on the smaller frame. "I feel all boxed in, like I'm riding a kid's bike."

"Let me make some adjustments," he said. Glynn raised the seat and changed the handlebar stem to a longer one.

Those slight changes made a huge difference. "This really feels comfortable. Way better than the other."

"Yeah," he replied, as if he knew it would. He then pulled out his odd-shaped ruler and measured the various angles of my body. "This is generally where you want to be. Your body looks more relaxed and less stressed. Of course, once we get your bike, we'll fine-tune it even more. Wanna take this one out back for a spin?"

A grin spread across my face.

We walked to the back of the store and he handed me a helmet that barely fit over my head. Once we stepped into the alley, Glynn handed me the bike and I took off, riding from one end of the alley to the other. The muscle spasms decreased in their intensity. I could've ridden all afternoon, but I figured that he probably had paying customers that required his attention.

"Thanks, that was great," I said, handing him the bike.

"I know you said you wanted to wait, but we can pick out the bike you want so that when you have the money, you can call me and order it."

That sounded reasonable enough. I was there; I had no other plans, so why not make the most of this opportunity. My stomach growled, but I ignored it.

I followed Glynn back to the corner of the store and we sat down in front of a computer. He clicked on a link, which took us to the dealer site for Trek Bikes, where we began selecting every component of a Trek Madone 5. I got to choose everything from the drivetrain to the handlebar tape and once the components were settled, I started picking the colors. When the design was finished, Glynn clicked on the "finish" button and showed me the price. Five thousand dollars.

      I hadn't planned on spending that much money. The bike that was wrecked in the accident only, only, cost three thousand five hundred dollars.

      "What do you think?" Glynn asked.

      "I like it."

      I like Porsche's and Ferrari's too, but that doesn't mean I can afford one.

      "I have an idea. How about we try the next model up, the Madone 6? We can change some of the components so that they match the 5 series, but you'd get a bike with the 6 series frame. I don't know what it would cost, but since you're not buying anything today, it might be fun."

      "Sure, why not?"

      And he was right. This was fun. Once more, Glynn guided me through the process of selecting the components and the colors. Ten minutes later, he printed out prototype number two, which turned out to be five hundred dollars more than prototype one. I stared at the two pictures. Forget the nightmares, I was going to ride a bike again. No question about it.

      While my brain salivated over the pictures, my mouth opened and uttered the following words, "If I ordered it today, how long before it got here?"

      "Ten to fourteen days."

      I paused, only briefly, before asking the next question. "How much of a deposit would I need to put down?"

      "Twenty percent."

      Before I could even calculate what that percentage might mean in actual dollars or how I might come up with the eighty percent in ten to fourteen days, the words, "Let's do it," flowed out of my mouth.

"Which one?"

"Prototype number two, the Trek Madone 6."

Perhaps the accident had ruptured something in my mental faculties thereby impairing my cognitive reasoning. I'd told Glynn that I had no intention of purchasing anything that day. Besides the lack of money, there were those nightmares. Then, in a fit of bike lust I committed to spending five thousand five hundred dollars on a new bike. At most, even with the settlement, I'd hoped to keep the cost of a new bike to less than four thousand. Maybe my brain hadn't healed like the rest of my body.

But forget the nightmares. I loved riding a bike and I wanted to keep on riding a bike. The nightmares could taunt me all they wanted.

And they would.

As for the money, I'd figure that out later.

Two hours after arriving at Richardson Bike Mart, I walked out of the store with a copy of an order for a customized Trek Madone 6, a receipt stating I'd put the eleven hundred dollar deposit on my credit card, and a statement that obligated me to pay the remaining forty four hundred dollar balance in two weeks. The words I'd uttered to Angela that morning rang in my ears, "Don't worry, I'm not going to spend any money."

I got in the car and called Angela. "Well, I'm not sure how this happened, but I just ordered a new bike."

"I trust you," she said, then she added, "and I knew you would."

On Friday morning the alarm went off at six and I dragged myself out of bed after having been tortured for the second straight night by nightmares. By day, I brushed them off as a minor inconvenience, something that wouldn't stop me, but in the darkness of night they'd scared me to the point of wondering whether I'd ever be able to get on a bike again.

Had I just wasted several thousand dollars on the purchase of a new bike? With only three hours sleep in each of the previous two nights, I was too exhausted to think about it.

At the gym for my first workout since the accident, I started with sit-ups and planks. During the four weeks I'd been sidelined on the couch eating cookies and brownies, I'd added a few pounds. Maybe five. Maybe a few more. All of it around the midsection. After working my core, I moved to a stationary bike. Based on the previous day's experience at the bike shop, I knew pedaling would hurt. I slid the white ear buds in and scrolled through the videos on my iPod until I found a cycling workout I'd downloaded from thesufferfest.com. I'd stumbled upon this website with its cycling training videos the year before. Along with workout instructions, the videos contained clips from professional cycling so that you could imagine yourself racing against the sport's best. Great music rounded out the workout. The sufferfest made indoor cycling enjoyable. Of the videos I had from the sufferfest, I selected *Heaven Knows I'm Miserable Now*. (This particular video, although still my favorite, is no longer available.) The title seemed appropriate for my state. After a brief warm-up, I spent five minutes chasing after Fabian Cancellara in the 2008 Olympics Road Race and then the workout switched to fifteen one minute intervals, one minute of all out effort followed by one minute of rest.

I cranked up the volume and increased the resistance as I followed the instructions on the screen. Ten minutes on a bike in the alley the previous day hadn't released the pent-up pain in my leg. Spasms shot up and down my left calf as I pedaled. I didn't feel as if I could continue. A month's inactivity had made my legs weak. Both thighs burned and my breathing was labored, but I completed the workout. My shirt and shorts were drenched with sweat and sticking to me. Apparently, dri-fit material has a maximum sweat quotient at which it can no longer wick away the moisture.

I felt great.

Josh, a friend from church, invited a few of us to attend a Texas Rangers baseball game in his company's suite. Even though the weatherman predicted a one hundred percent chance of heavy thunderstorms for the entire night, we still went to the stadium. Once we made it to the confines of the suite, we were free from the rain. We sat in the dry and air-conditioned comfort of the room, eating free hot dogs, chicken tenders, and nachos, drinking free Cokes and Sprites, while watching TV on one of the three big screens.

Somebody stopped on a channel that was showing a highlight montage from Michael Jordan's career. I'd first encountered Jordan as a seventh-grader when I sat on the living room floor at my Dad's house and watched this skinny freshman hit the game-winning jump shot for North Carolina in the championship game. When I got home from school the next day, I spent the afternoon imitating that very same shot. The next season I watched North Carolina every time they were on TV and when Jordan played in the 1984 Olympics I never missed a game. I couldn't have been happier when the Chicago Bulls drafted him. I might've been happier if my hometown team, the San Antonio Spurs, had been able to draft him, but WGN telecast every Bulls game, which meant that I wouldn't miss a single Jordan game. And I didn't.

The highlights ended and Jordan was introduced. He stood on the stage and began his induction speech into the Basketball Hall of Fame. Someone un-muted the volume so we could hear the speech. Jordan mentioned every person, or so it seemed, who'd ever slighted him on the basketball court, reminding everyone that he used those slights, perceived or real, as the driving motivation to become one of the best basketball players ever.

When Jordan finished his speech, someone muted the TV again and changed the channel to a Friday night college football game. Rain continued to drench the field and a few guys wondered when the game might be cancelled.

I kept thinking about Jordan's speech, how he motivated himself to be better. I felt trapped in a circle that I wanted to break out of. I wanted to ride, but then I was afraid to ride. I didn't care about the nightmares, but then the nightmares frightened me. If only there had been someone telling me that I couldn't or shouldn't get back on a bike again, then I could focus on proving him or her wrong. But there wasn't. Nobody cared. I wasn't a professional cyclist or even an amateur racer. I was just some guy who enjoyed the sport and the exercise. It made no difference to the world if I ever rode a bike again.

The only opponent I faced stared back at me in the mirror and he proved to be a much harder foe than anyone I'd ever faced. Fear was on his side.

After one particular workout, my leg muscles felt tight and stiff so I decided to spend some time stretching. First, I worked at stretching my hamstrings. I lifted one leg on top of a railing that was level to my hip and slowly leaned forward over this outstretched leg. I stopped, changed legs, and stretched the other hamstring. Next, I decided to work on my quadriceps. I swung my left leg up behind me, grabbed a hold of my ankle, and pulled it back towards me. A sharp pain ripped through my calf and I let go of my leg. I felt the pain in the exact spot where my divot fracture had been. A glutton for punishment, maybe even a fool, I tried the same maneuver again, this time slower. I felt the pain again, yet I didn't release my foot immediately. I held on for a few seconds longer before I let go. The pain felt like the bone was getting ready to snap.

I attempted the same quadriceps stretch on the right leg, but experienced no pain. I wondered if I'd injured myself or if the attempts at stretching had revealed that the leg hadn't fully healed. I walked around the gym, bouncing up and down, lightly jumping, to see if I experienced any more pain. None came.

The pain could be anything, I told myself. It could be my mind playing tricks on me. It might be scar tissue from the injury. I didn't want to call the doctor. If I made an appointment, I'd have to call Mick and let him know. If my attorney knew, then he'd want to postpone proposing any settlement with Dr. Pepper. Mick might want me to see another doctor for a second opinion. I'd have to make an appointment, get new x-rays, and go through the whole process again. Meanwhile, my bike would be arriving any day. I decided to do nothing. If I experienced the pain while engaged in any other activities besides stretching, then I'd call Dr. Shane. Otherwise, I'd continue on like nothing had happened.

    A Richardson Bike Mart employee called me on a Monday, ten days after I'd placed my order. "Your bike is here and ready for pickup." Unfortunately, I couldn't get there until Thursday to pick it up, the downside of buying a bike from a store an hour away. On the bright side, the three extra days would give me time to figure out how I was going to come up with the money for the outstanding balance.
    On the Trek website, I discovered that they were offering zero percent financing for six months. If I made the minimum monthly payments on time and paid the balance within six months, I wouldn't owe any interest. If I was late or didn't pay off the balance, I'd be charged with all the accrued interest. As dire as the terms might be, their financing would put the bike in my hands and give me six months to find the money. Maybe Dr. Pepper would have settled by then.
    Then there were the nightmares. They'd tormented me for a couple of nights after the purchase of the bike and then left me alone. The night before I went to pick up the bike, they returned once more and thrashed me for most of the night. In the morning I wondered what would it take to get rid of them.

I arrived at Richardson Bike Mart and found Glynn in the back corner securing my new bike to a trainer. I'd emailed him on Tuesday to let him know I'd be there on Thursday at twelve-thirty. I was five minutes early. My new bike, black and gray with thin red stripes looked sleeker than the pictures on the Trek website. I changed into my bike shorts and jersey for the bike fit.

When I purchased my first bike, no one mentioned a thing about a bike fit. The extent of the consultation was the employee's question of "How does it feel?" after my test ride. I later complained to a fellow cyclist that my shoulders were always hurting while riding.

"Did you get a bike fit?" he asked.

"A what? I'm not some sort of racer or anything." I figured that you bought what felt comfortable and kept adjusting the seat height until it was perfect. Besides, I'd expected that there would be, there should be, some discomfort.

"Go get a bike fit," he said.

I went back to the bike store, explained my aches and pains, and they put my bike and me on a trainer. The employee switched the stem to a shorter one, which I didn't know they could do, and raised the seat a little. Those little adjustments eliminated my aches and pains, making me a believer in a bike fit.

"Just start pedaling at a nice relaxed pace," Glynn instructed. He pulled out the strange looking ruler and checked the angle of my upper body. "Looks good." Then, he sat down in a chair next to me, warning me beforehand that he would be stopping my foot in mid-pedal. "Hold it there," he said when he'd grabbed my foot. He held a piece of string against my kneecap with a weight the size of a small rock at the bottom. "Stand up for a minute." I moved and he adjusted the seat height. He then re-checked the measurements.

"How's it feel?" he asked.

"Good." An understatement on my part. It felt great, fantastic, and awesome. Of course, those feelings could also have been the result of getting a new toy rather than being properly aligned to my bike.

I made the financing arrangements with Glynn while one of the service technicians went over the bike one last time, checking cables and bolts. I'd skipped lunch to arrive at the store by twelve-thirty and it was nearing two o'clock. My stomach registered its need for food and the encroaching dark clouds eliminated the possibility of an afternoon bike ride. I secured the bike to the rack on my car, but without the lock since I'd forgotten it at home. I drove across the parking lot to Qdoba and parked next to the handicapped spot so I could keep an eye on my brand new unlocked bike. While ordering my burrito, I kept glancing over my shoulder for any suspicious activity near my car.

Rain, Dallas highways, and an ensuing rush hour do not make for pleasant driving conditions. A one-hour commute can easily turn into a two or three hour drive. With a rainstorm approaching, I finished my lunch in just a few bites. I did not want to get stuck in Dallas traffic. Unfortunately, the highways were already congested so I drove with both hands gripping the steering wheel. I was worried that someone might clip the car from the side or worse yet rear-end me and damage my new bike. A hand only left the steering wheel when I needed to honk the horn or gesture at someone who'd gotten too close to me.

The drive in the drizzling rain took an hour and a half. Just as I turned into my neighborhood, a thunderstorm erupted. I parked in the garage and leaned the bike against the car where I dried it off and checked for any scratches or chipped paint. After not finding any, I put the bike away and watched the rain.

The nightmares hounded me on Thursday and Friday. When I woke up on Saturday morning, I calculated that I'd been averaging three hours of sleep for the past few nights.

That day, September twenty-sixth, would be the day, my first ride on the new bike, and my first ride since the accident. I lay there in bed, thinking about the other things I had to do that day, call Dad for his birthday, go to the store, and mow the yard.

Prior to the accident, a Saturday morning bike commenced at the first break of light. That morning, the sun had already been up for an hour. I got out of bed and went downstairs to toast frozen waffles for Samuel and myself. While Samuel and I ate breakfast, I peppered him with questions about his plans for the day ("Play"), his choice for a Halloween costume ("Tigger"), any toys he might want for Christmas (too many to list), and how did he like his pre-K class ("No fun!").

"Are we done yet?" he interjected before I could fire off another question.

"Just one more thing," I said.

"I just wanna go play."

"In a minute."

Angela walked in the kitchen with her hair pulled back into a ponytail wearing jeans and a t-shirt. "Aren't you going to ride your new bike today?"

"Yeah."

"When?"

"This morning."

Samuel used Angela's questions as a diversionary tactic to jump down from the table and run from the room. She went to the laundry room while I put our plates in the dishwasher and then went upstairs to change clothes. I remembered that I needed to file the bike receipt, but when I went into the office I saw a whole stack of documents and receipts that needed filing so I busied myself with that task. When I finished, I walked towards our bedroom but saw Samuel playing in his room.

"Whatcha doing, buddy?"

"Playing."

him. I sat down on the floor and began playing cars with him. Angela came and stopped in the doorway of Samuel's room. "I thought you were going riding?"

"I am."

Samuel once more used the distraction created by Angela to vacate the room, leaving his toys and me behind. Alone again, I changed into my cycling clothes and prepared to leave. I put on my new helmet, but then realized that I hadn't adjusted the straps. That took me thirty minutes. I stopped at the stairs to tell Angela I was leaving on my bike ride.

"By the way, do we have any plans tonight?" I asked.

"Do you want to go ride your bike?" she quizzed.

"Of course," I replied.

Eventually. Perhaps. At some point. Maybe today. Theoretically, I did. Realistically, I didn't. A stream of butterflies fluttered in my stomach every time I thought of getting on that bike, but I didn't want to admit my fears to her. If I delayed any longer, she'd have me figured out, if she hadn't already. I half-smiled, grabbed my water bottles, and headed to the garage.

She yelled my name and I turned back around. I hoped that she might tell me not to get on that bike. Instead, she showed me her cellphone. "I have it with me. Just in case."

That didn't help at all. She'd given my fears a steroid shot. A double shot at that. One thought reverberated in my head, "I hope I don't die."

After inflating the tires, I took one last look at the house, as if it might be the last time I might ever see it, and then I rode down the driveway. At first, I limited myself to our neighborhood streets as I checked the gears and the brakes to make sure they were working fine. I nodded at the few people I saw standing outside in their driveways and yards. I started to relax and enjoy myself.

I merged onto a street with more traffic in the neighborhood. Prior to the accident, I'd always noticed cars when riding. I watched for them, particularly when approaching intersections or passing driveways, but rarely did I hear a car approaching from behind unless the engine was loud. On this first ride, I heard every single vehicle. If twenty or thirty seconds passed without me hearing a car, I turned around and checked for any oncoming traffic. When a car did approach, my hands gripped the handlebars tighter while my heart rate increased and my spine stiffened. My pedaling would slow until the car passed. My neck and shoulder grew stiff. The relaxation and enjoyment of riding a bike had left.

I rode thirty minutes south of our house where I could begin riding on some deserted country roads. Ten minutes later, I felt as if my knees were about to hit the handlebars.

I looked down and noticed that I couldn't fully extend my legs on the downward extension of my pedal stroke. My seat had slid down. I turned into a church parking lot and inspected the bike, where I discovered that the seat post had slipped all the way down, leaving the seat resting just above the frame. The bolt was loose so I pulled the seat up and tightened the bolt with an Allen wrench I had in my seat bag. I hadn't marked the seat post prior to riding, so I guessed as to where Glynn had set it during my bike fit.

Forty minutes ought to be a good spot for me to turnaround on my first day, I thought. It wouldn't make for a very long ride, but it was a start. My decision was helped by the fact that I hadn't enjoyed much of the ride.

As I continued home, the seat continued to slide down. Twice, I stopped, re-raised it, and re-tightened the bolt. The third time it slipped down, I left it there and continued riding the bike like it was. I convinced myself that this bike was defective. I'd have to make the hour long drive back to Dallas and hope they wouldn't have to ship it back to the manufacturer. Just my luck. I finally got a new bike and it was damaged. The thoughts of a malfunctioning bike pushed out all thoughts of getting hit by a vehicle.

I took my bike back to Richardson Bike Mart that afternoon. Glynn re-adjusted the seat and then applied carbon fiber glue to the seat post. "That should hold it," he declared. And it did.

Prior to the accident, I seized every opportunity to ride my bike, sometimes re-arranging my schedule so that I'd have large blocks of time to go for a ride. At other times, if I found forty-five free minutes, I hurried to make the most of that time on the bike. If clouds gathered and the radar showed precipitation, I stuffed a rain jacket in one of the back jersey pockets before I left and hoped I could out sprint the rain.

Yet now, I hesitated to get on a bike, sometimes even looking for excuses not to go for a ride. It might rain. It was too windy. It was too close to school letting out or rush hour starting.

I had to force myself to go. It would be a colossal waste of money not to ride this bike. And think of the insurance settlement negotiations, I needed to know that my body had completely healed before signing any waiver of liability. Only by riding a bike would I know the answer to that question.

So I went, usually by myself. I liked riding alone, letting my thoughts roam, stopping when I wanted, accelerating when I wanted to push the pace. There were a group of friends I rode with from time to time, and I liked the change of pace, but the solitary nature of a man and two wheels appealed to me. Yet when I rode alone, post-accident, I worried about being hit again. The only time I dropped those thoughts was when I went with others. Either the company or the conversation or some combination of the two forced my brain to concentrate on something else.

Adding to the weight were the nightmares that would not leave. We'd engaged, unwillingly on my part, in an on-again, off-again relationship and since the purchase of a new bike, we were in an on-again phase.

For the first time, the details of the nightmare had changed. The nightmare always began with me at home in the same black bibs and red jersey on my old red bike. I rode through the surrounding streets, but instead of turning right on Pleasant Ridge I continued straight up a short steep hill. The road changed from four lanes to a two-lane overpass that extended over six lanes of interstate. I'd travelled across this overpass hundreds of times. In my nightmare, I reach the top of the hill and begin across this overpass. At the halfway point, a truck strikes me from behind. This time, instead of being tossed into the grass, I am catapulted over the knee high concrete barrier and into the oncoming interstate traffic. Just before impact, I am jolted awake. My heart pounds and I struggle to catch my breath.

After that new nightmare, I avoided this overpass. Whereas, I'd always gone across it on my longer rides, I searched out a different overpass, one with actual bike lanes. The fact that the nightmares had changed from haunting me with a past event to scaring me with a potential future accident started to drain the last bits of desire I possessed to ride a bike.

Even though it had rained all morning and dark clouds remained, I forced myself to get on my bike. I checked the weather radar and the rain had moved on. But, I countered, the streets were still wet. Going to the gym would be a better idea. Safer. I wouldn't listen to reason. I was going riding. No matter what.

Once on the road, I pedaled cautiously, wary of the cars all around me. I couldn't keep turning my head to look behind me, as had become my new habit. On a dry surface you can turn or lean to the left or to the right without fear, but on a wet surface, half that same lean will send you sliding across the road. Because the streets were wet, I feared that if I turned my head too quickly I might inadvertently yank the handlebars, which might cause the tires to slip out from under me, thereby causing an accident.

After thirty minutes, I escaped the city streets to some less-travelled country roads. The roads had yet to dry off and the clouds threatened rain, despite what the radar had shown. I started to relax and pedal a little faster. The sound of a diesel engine, similar to that of an eighteen-wheeler, came up behind me. Because there were so many natural gas wells in the area, it wasn't uncommon to encounter an eighteen-wheeler on these two-lane roads. The engine lumbered and choked behind me. I slowed my speed while I tightened my grip on the handlebars. I wanted to turn and see how close he might be but I feared that I might slip and fall.

I kept pedaling and he stayed behind me. To the right of the road was a ditch, so I had no choice but to keep going. "Please don't kill me. Please don't let me die." Nobody would be able to hear me talking to myself over the noise of his engine. I gripped the handlebars even tighter.

The engine grew louder as if the truck were directly behind me. I glanced out of the corner of my eye but I still couldn't see the vehicle's approach. Some drivers, maybe out of deference or maybe out of their own fear of hitting a cyclist, will stay behind a bike rider rather than passing him. But we were on a two-lane country road with no oncoming traffic. There was plenty of room for him to pass me.

My heart pounded. "Come on," I yelled, "Just go around me!" I considered lifting one of my hands off the handlebars and waving him past, but I was too close to the edge of the road. One little bump or jitter of my hand and I might send myself sprawling into the ditch.

Should've gone to the gym instead.

"Come on!" This truck wasn't passing me. I focused on riding in a straight line so that if he did decide to pass me he wouldn't hit me. The engine coughed and gurgled, getting louder and louder, closer and closer.

"Go!"

We rounded a bend and I spotted a gravel driveway twenty yards ahead on the right. I sped up and headed for it. I veered into the driveway and slammed on the brakes. I turned to glare at this driver, maybe to raise my hands in defiance as well. Maybe to yell at him as he passed. But when I turned to look for this monster of an eighteen-wheeler, it wasn't there. I still heard the laboring of an engine, but it didn't belong to a truck or even a car.

The sounds of this evil gurgling, lumbering, coughing engine emanated from a train fifty yards to my left as it wheezed along the railroad tracks. I smiled. I leaned over and rested my head on the top of the handlebars. Laughter overtook me. If any car had driven past me at that moment, I would've looked quite foolish bent over my bike laughing. I gathered myself and raised my head off of the handlebars. "It's time...it's time to get over it." I pushed off the gravel driveway, clipped my cleats into the pedals, and kept riding.

The accident had not been my fault. I'd done everything I could, but I couldn't control someone else's actions. I had no power over whether or not I might get hit again.

I never had another nightmare.

SEVEN
SETTLING THE BILL

So it took four weeks of being confined to a walking boot, six weeks of pushing myself to ride a bike, and one imagined encounter with an eighteen-wheeler to get my life back. I spent less time in the gym and more time on an actual bike.

And then a bill collector called.

"I never received a bill from North Texas Ambulatory Services," I said.

He verified my address and told me that a statement had been mailed to me twice. Since the bill had gone unpaid, my account had been turned over to a debt collector.

"I'm not paying a bill when I never received a bill."

"We'll send another one to you and follow up with a phone call in ten business days."

Though I hadn't received this particular bill, I'd received a host of others. Those along with payments for my Ferrari of a bike loomed in the near future. Never having been a party to a personal injury case, I didn't know how long it would take to negotiate a settlement with Dr. Pepper. Given the weight of evidence in my favor, I imagined the process would go quickly. I thought wrong.

I sent Mick a stack of documents: pictures of my injuries, pictures of the damaged bike, copies of my medical bills, copies of the doctor's notes, and the journal noting my emotional state throughout the entire process. He prepared a letter for Dr. Pepper's insurance adjustor outlining our case along with these documents requesting a dollar amount to settle the matter. After three weeks, when he hadn't heard from the adjustor, he followed up with a phone call.

"We need additional time to evaluate your request," they said.

Additional time? As for personal injury cases, mine was fairly simple and straightforward. Their employee had been at fault by his own admission, I'd healed without any lingering side effects (other than the scar that extended the entire length of my right arm and the one on my face where I'd gotten stitches), property had been damaged, and I wasn't requesting a seven-figure settlement. The merits of the case were beyond question. Cut me a check.

Mick called the adjustor a week later, who said she'd sent the packet to the Dallas offices of Dr. Pepper to verify the accuracy of the incident. It seemed to me as though they might be giving us the run around, as if they didn't want to pay. Those thoughts were confirmed in my mind ten days later when the adjustor could no longer find the documents we'd sent them. Mick resent them to the adjustor.

Perhaps this was a negotiating ploy on their part. Stall, delay, and stall. Maybe they thought that I'd become desperate enough to take whatever dollar amount they offered me. My instructions to Mick were clear. "I don't care how long it takes. I can wait them out. I want a fair settlement."

Medical bills arrived in the mail marked "Past Due." More doctors and their offices turned my account over to debt collectors, who sent notices and left voicemails. I ignored calls from unknown numbers. The one or two collectors that I spoke with when I mistakenly answered the phone warned me of the dire consequences that this could do to my credit rating. I told them, "I could care less about my credit. You'll get the money when I have the money." I never mentioned to them that the money would be coming from a Fortune 500 company.

A week and a half before Christmas, Mick called me after having spoken with the adjustor again. "She said that she wouldn't be able to even look at your claim until after the first of the year. I think they're stalling. My advice is that we need to sue them to get their attention. It may end up in court or this may drive them to start negotiating. But this is your case. If you want to wait a little longer, then we can wait."

"Sue them."

After the adjustor was served two days later, she managed to locate my claim packet and review its contents. She called Mick and they began negotiating a settlement. When they'd arrived at a number, he called me for my approval. It wasn't enough for me to retire, not even close to that, but the medical bills and bike would be paid for and I'd have a little bit left over to put in savings.

With an agreement, I figured that a check would be arriving within the week. The adjustor insisted that in order for her to comply with her company's rules, she would need to send two separate checks, one for medical bills and mental anguish and a separate check for the property damage. The first check arrived a month after we'd settled and the second check three months later. Mick had to threaten to re-file the lawsuit to get her to send the second check.

When I deposited the checks, I realized one thing. Throughout the entire ordeal, from the first day of the accident to the day we settled, no one from Dr. Pepper ever contacted me. They never checked to see how I was doing or even to apologize for the havoc they'd wreaked on my life.

When people hear about the accident, once they get over the shock that I'm alive, that I continue to ride a bike, after they've looked at the scar that extends along my right arm, and have asked about the financial settlement, they ask, "Why do you think it happened?" They want to know what purpose there was in this accident. Did I learn something? I don't know if it's because I'm a minister and studied religion in college or if they ask these sorts of questions to everyone they know who's been through such pain, but they ask me.

Some people emerge from traumatic events a different person with a renewed vision for their lives or some passion to help those who encounter similar fates as themselves. I suspect that some people want to hear that I've become more attentive to Angela and Samuel. Or maybe that I sought out those I'd wronged and offended and made my peace. If not that, then maybe I learned to be at peace with myself. Or better yet, I glimpsed into the frailty of life and emerged a more determined and focused person.

"Why?" they press, "Why the pain, why the suffering, why the accident?"

I cannot answer for others, only for myself. Others might find great significance or life change or even answers for their pain. My answer is "I don't know why."

I can see with their downcast eyes and slumped shoulders that my answer has let them down. After all, I'm a minister, someone whose job it is to reach into the deep wells of thinking and prayer and find the answers to these difficult questions. It's as if I have handed them an empty bucket. When I have given this answer, some have retorted with suggestions on how they think my life should've been changed by this accident.

To say, "I don't know why," means that I'm not in control. Even though I'm a decent person, at least I think I am, a guy who walked away from a career with an investment firm to work for a church, who loves his family and wants to help people, bad things will even happen to me. No one is immune. I can't control the actions of the driver behind me. I can't control anyone or anything. And yet, with every illness or accident or unkind act towards me I must learn this lesson over and over again. I'm not in control.

Yet, in the midst of these dreadful events, these dark clouds, there are glimpses of light, rainbows on the horizon that remind me of the goodness that still exists. They can be what some might dismiss as little things, meaningless gestures, or unimportant conversations. But those little, meaningless, unimportant things were the most significant things that took place in my pain. People reaching out to you can be the difference between you dying and surviving. A little thing like someone making dinner for my family when I couldn't cook. A little thing like my friend Mike buying me a book on biking. A text or a phone call to see if I needed anything or to make sure I was doing okay. Or a guy at church who walked up to me a few weeks after the accident and said, "You have to get back on your bike. You have to."

Fear leaned on me, pushing with all of its strength, trying to mold me into a different person. More often than not, I wanted to yield to its pressures. It would be so easy to cave and give in, to never get on a bike again. The road fear offered was wide and smooth, free of the things that might knock me over. The other road, the one without answers, the one with things that taunted me at night invading my dreams, the one with steep hills and the sounds of eighteen-wheelers threatening to crush me from behind, was the more difficult way. But it was the road I knew and I wanted to get back there. There were no signposts telling me I had almost arrived, rather the posted signs said, "Keep going."

There may be more hills, perhaps even diversions and roadblocks, on this road. There might even be more accidents. I will always be able to see a path to the other road. But I want to stay on this one, confronting my fears and worries, but never doing so alone. The easy road offered by fear is filled with people, but it is lonely. The road I am traveling is less populated, but I am never alone. A hand passes me a water bottle, another gives me a push on the back, and another gives me a thumbs-up sign.

Perhaps I learned a few things after all.

ACKNOWLEDGEMENTS

To every person who helped me in my recovery, both those who were mentioned and those who were not, I owe you a tremendous thank you. My road back would've been a thousand times tougher without you.

To the witnesses of the accident, those who could've kept on going, but stopped and called 911 and later spoke with the police, thank you. We've never met and you may never read these words, but I am forever grateful to you.

Although I dish a fair bit of sarcasm towards some medical professionals, my words come from the viewpoint of a patient in pain. You were doing your job to the best of your abilities and my recovery shows that you knew what you were doing, despite my doubts.

Thank you to readers of my blog, **www.thisischrisdikes.wordpress.com**, who offered feedback on earlier versions of this narrative. Your comments continue to inspire me.

To the ninth grade English teacher at Reagan High School in Austin, Texas (in the fall of 1983, I think), whose name I can't remember, who encouraged me to write, thank you. Your words sparked something within me and I've been hooked on the bug of stringing words together every since.

To my cycling friends, I look forward to many more rides together.

None of this would be possible without Angela and Samuel. Samuel puts the smile on my face each and every day. As for Angela, I cannot imagine where or what or who I would be without her in my life. She is my wife, my best friend, and even my nurse. She is perfect for me.

ABOUT THE AUTHOR

Chris Dikes was born in San Antonio, Texas and now lives in Arlington, Texas with his wife and son. He is a graduate of Hardin-Simmons University. Chris works as an Associate Pastor at CrossRoads of Arlington Church. *The Accident: A Bike, A Truck, and A Train* is his first book.

When he's not riding his bike, he can be found online at www.thisischrisdikes.wordpress.com.

Made in the USA
Charleston, SC
22 January 2012